URBANISM AND THE CHANGING
CANADIAN SOCIETY

In honour of

CHARLES ALLAN ASHLEY

Professor of Accounting, University of Toronto
1941–1945

Professor of Commerce
1945–

Chairman of the Department of Political Economy
1952, 1959–1961

URBANISM AND THE CHANGING CANADIAN SOCIETY

EDITED BY

S. D. Clark

UNIVERSITY OF TORONTO PRESS

Introduction

IT IS APPROPRIATE that this volume be dedicated to Professor C. A. Ashley. It was his suggestion that led to the idea of bringing together a volume of essays written by members of the sociology staff of the University of Toronto. The essays were written and the volume prepared for publication during the period when he was chairman of the Department of Political Economy. He has been a good friend of sociology.

The volume might be thought to have several purposes but the one it serves best perhaps is the marking of the coming of age of sociology in the University of Toronto. It is now just a little more than twenty-five years since the honours course in sociology was established in this university. To anyone not familiar with the thinking in the University at the time, it might appear strange that the course was set up before there was a single person on the staff to teach sociology, and when provision for its teaching was made it was by bringing over on a part-time basis a member of the staff of anthropology. But among the founders of the course, sociology was not thought of as an independent area of study; rather it was conceived of as a distinctive grouping of a number of different areas: economics, political science, philosophy, history, psychology, anthropology, and zoology. The honours course in sociology of these first few years was a truly excellent programme of study even though it contained only the barest minimum of instruction in sociology as such.

To the late Professor E. J. Urwick belongs the credit for seeing the need in this university for an honours course in sociology, for bringing the course into being and for guiding its development in the first years after its establishment. Though Professor Urwick was never prepared to accept the claims of sociology as a science, and he would take no title for himself other than that of social philosopher, he greatly furthered its advance by bringing to bear upon his teachings about society a strong human interest in people and concern for their welfare. Sociology at Toronto owes much to him.

It owes much as well to Professor C. W. M. Hart who first taught what was called sociology in this university. If Professor Urwick had doubts about the claims of sociology as a science, those doubts were not shared by Professor Hart. Though an anthropologist by training, Hart had been brought close to the great master of sociology, Emile Durkheim, through Radcliffe-Brown, and it was a rigorously positivistic and functionally oriented sociology which he introduced to his students at Toronto. There were few of these students whose thinking was not profoundly affected by his teachings. It was he who truly pioneered instruction in sociology in this university.

It is easy to become nostalgic about those early years when I joined Hart as a member of the Toronto staff of sociology. It was something of a struggle, but then as today sociology had many good friends, not the least of whom was the late Dean H. A. Innis, and as part of the Department of Political Economy, it prospered through its close and strengthening ties with economics and political science. Sociology never suffered at Toronto, as it has in some other universities, from being isolated from its sister social science disciplines.

Whatever doubts may have persisted, however, about whether there was a separate science of sociology, the development of the past several years has very fully resolved them. Work in sociology has grown enormously not only at the University of Toronto but throughout Canada. At the time sociology was introduced at Toronto, only McGill among the Canadian universities seriously offered instruction in it. Today there is scarcely a university in Canada which does not offer a substantial programme of training in the field. The development of sociology in these other Canadian centres of learning has done much to further its development in this university.

This little volume is intended to convey some idea of what is going on in sociology at the University of Toronto. The essays do not have the nature of research reports, but they do offer some hint of the main interests and fields of work of their authors. Because they do, there can be no great unity in the volume as a whole. There is an indication of a concentration upon certain kinds of problems, largely having to do with urban growth and the changing structure of Canadian society, and it is this focus of interest which justifies the title given to the volume. But sociologists are nothing if they are not individualists, and this collection of essays gives best expression not to the sameness but to the variety of interests represented by the authors.

In the essay by Professor Keyfitz is reflected an interest in popula-

tion which is not unrelated to a more general interest in the sociology
of underdeveloped countries. From her earlier study of an Alberta
rural community, Professor Burnet has turned to a concern with the
relationship of moral values to the changing structure of the Canadian community and here fastens attention on the impact of urban
growth upon such values. An interest of Professor Mann (on the
staff of Ontario Agricultural College affiliated with the University
of Toronto) in the informal social structure of downtown urban
areas has grown naturally out of an earlier interest in sectarian
religious phenomena. For Professor Hall, an interest in the sociology
of the professions has led to a general interest in the sociology of
work. For Professor Giffen, on the other hand, study of the legal
profession has led to an interest in such deviant forms of behaviour
as crime and juvenile delinquency. Professor Zakuta has moved from
a particular interest in the structure of the C.C.F. party to a general
interest in the sociology of social institutions and social movements.
My own interest in suburban development has grown naturally out
of a general interest in the changing structure of the Canadian community.

What is offered here can scarcely be thought of as an introduction
to sociology. It can be hoped, however, that the volume will serve
to introduce the student to some of the kinds of problems sociologists are thinking about. It is perhaps not unbecoming to hope as
well that it will make better known to the student of sociology the
members of the sociology staff of the University of Toronto. No idle
claims of its accomplishments can do for sociology what can be done
by the demonstration of solid achievement.

                                                    S. D. CLARK

Contents

URBANISM AND THE CHANGING
CANADIAN SOCIETY

The
Changing Canadian Population[1]

N. KEYFITZ

THIS ESSAY will say something about the way in which the population of Canada reached its present number and spatial distribution, analyse the components of past growth, and comment on how these may operate in the future. It will show that for Canada as for all nations it is the birth rate which is decisive in determining the rate of increase and constitution of population, and it will trace the evolution of our birth rate from the high levels characteristic of the frontier to the lower rates of the industrial city. The main proposition will be that family size is becoming more and more a matter of personal choice and less and less dictated by nature. Paradoxically, the more the size of the family is subject to private decisions of couples the more the family approaches a standard number; all statistically recognizable groups—French and English, city and country, rich and poor—seem to be approaching a three-child norm. Evidently the choices of individuals approximate more completely to a mean value than do the vagaries of nature.

Over-all Increase

The hundredth anniversary of Confederation will be celebrated on July 1, 1967, by about 20,800,000 residents of Canada. The increase from 3.5 million in 1867 will have been slightly more than sixfold during the hundred year period, an average increase of 1.8 per cent per year, a doubling on the average every forty years. This exceeds the fourfold increase of the population of England and Wales during the nineteenth century, and that of most of the countries of Europe during their transition from high to low birth and death rates. It is however slightly slower than the increase shown by the United States

[1] I am grateful for valuable assistance from A. H. Le Neveu of the Census Division of the Dominion Bureau of Statistics in the statistical portions of this paper.

during the same period. Up to about the time of Confederation, the area that is now Canada had approximately one-tenth the population of the United States; we dropped to about 7 per cent of the United States population in 1901. Although we have been increasing relatively faster ever since, it will be some years at present rates of growth before we again reach one-tenth of the population of the United States.

Figures for the decade 1950-60 show the contemporary pattern of Canadian and United States growth. The United States census of 1960 will probably count about 180 million persons as against the 150 million of 1950. This 30 million increase for the ten-year period is only about seven times the Canadian increase. The greater proportional increase for Canada is due partly to a higher birth rate, partly to more immigrants. If the United States had our twenty-eight births per thousand instead of its twenty-five, its increase in the decade would have been higher by about 5 million persons.

Spatial Distribution

The over-all Canadian growth figures are not applicable to individual provinces and still less to areas within provinces. We must think of our population as in motion, with tides of people flowing this way and that, often filling new stretches, sometimes retreating from long-settled country-sides. A population history of Canada would have as a constant theme the way in which the perception of natural resources in one place and then another was responsible for the ebb and flow of population. Sometimes, however, the shift is in the need for labour on given resources as technology changes. As fishing, farming, mining, and lumbering on the Atlantic coast have become more mechanized, their labour force leaves for Central Canada and the United States where the equipment is made for these and other industries.

During the first forty years of the century, Prince Edward Island lost a number of people more than equal to its excess of births over deaths, and the number of its inhabitants declined steadily from 103,000 in 1901 to 88,000 in 1931. The exception was the 1930's when opportunity fell off so sharply in Central Canada that not only was there little incentive to leave the Island but some of those who had left earlier were driven back. The consistent direction of movement has been away from all three of the older Maritime provinces in recent years; they lost by migration 5,000 persons in 1931-41, 93,000 in 1941-51, and 40,000 in 1951-56.[2]

[2] *Canada Year Book*, 1959, p. 163.

British Columbia, on the other hand, has grown rapidly by attracting Canadians from other provinces and immigrants who have come to Canada from abroad. In no census of this century has it failed to show a greater increase from the preceding one than the country as a whole. Its growth has been parallel to that of California, attracting those industries which can afford to take account of climate, as well as those that use the products of its forests, mines, and fisheries and in which it is an advantage to be close to the point where their goods are shipped out of the country. The provinces in between have been less consistent: Ontario, and to a much smaller degree Quebec, lost to the Prairies before World War I and gained from the Prairies during and after the 1930's.

It is probably sound to regard moves among provinces, like those of Canadians to the United States, as essentially a movement to cities. City-ward migration has characterized our whole history. Thus a hundred years ago the population called urban was a very small part of the total; in 1956 it was 58 per cent on the census definition (including all incorporated places however small). Incorporated places of over 1,000 population contained 50.9 per cent of the total in 1941, 53.6 per cent in 1951, and 54.99 per cent in 1956.[3] Cities are increasing their share of the population of the country by almost 3 per cent per decade. If this pace continues until 1980, some two-thirds of the population will be urban.

Shifts from Agriculture to Industry

The above population figures are indicative of a response to the technical revolution in agriculture, on which light is thrown by the simple comparison of personnel and production during the past three decades. The invaluable *Output, Labour and Capital in the Canadian Economy* shows that in 1926 the agricultural labour force numbered 1,181,000;[4] this number rose with the agricultural exports of the prosperous twenties to a peak of 1,225,000 in 1928, fell to a low of 1,140,000 in 1931, and then started to rise again. The rise of the 1930's was due rather to people taking refuge on farms from city unemployment than to their being drawn by the labour needs of farm production, and so was bound to be temporary. In the depression the farm labour force reached a 1939 peak of 1,293,000, and

[3] *Canada Year Book*, 1959, p. 147.
[4] Wm. C. Hood and Anthony Scott, *Output, Labour and Capital in the Canadian Economy*, Royal Commission on Canada's Economic Prospects (Ottawa, 1957), p. 196.

this may well turn out to have been the all-time high no matter how much Canada grows. The 1940's and 1950's saw a steady decline to 725,000 in 1958.[5]

While the 1958 labour figure is down by 44 per cent from the 1939 figure, output has increased rapidly. Thus total farm cash income stood at $712 million in 1939 and at $2,787 million in 1958.[6] For purposes of assessing the volume change implied here, one might refer to the doubling in the cost of living index (63.2 to 125.1) in the same period;[7] the index of prices of commodities and services used by farmers increased from 99.4 in 1939 to 242.7 in 1958.[8] The Dominion Bureau of Statistics has worked out a direct measure of volume which showed 1956 at a high point fully 69 per cent above 1935-39;[9] in 1957, volume dropped to only 30 per cent above 1935-39. But we need not follow crop fluctuations. For our purpose it suffices to think of the last five years as showing half again as much output as 1935-39 with one-third less labour force. In the same period—the late thirties to late fifties—the labour force in business (as defined by Hood and Scott) increased by about 50 per cent and that in government doubled. The process whereby the ratio of business to agricultural labour force went from 2 : 1 in 1940 to nearly 5 : 1 in 1955[10] may be expected to continue into the future, and Hood and Scott's projections work out to a ratio of over 10 : 1 in 1980. The farmer seems to be disappearing under his mountainous production.

Components of Over-all Increase in Population

As a preliminary to more detailed study, one would like to know exactly how many people were born, died, immigrated, and emigrated, into and from the present area of Canada during Canadian history. Although on the basis of such figures one could not say exactly how much of our growth was due to natural increase and how much was due to migration, one would at least have a basis for eliminating some theories; one could also study trends and fluctuations in the rates of birth and migration, and so make a start in the assessing of the causes of fluctuations.

[5] *Canadian Statistical Review*, 1959 Supplement, p. 35.
[6] *Canadian Statistical Review*, 1959, p. 105. The figures given here are the quarterly averages multiplied by 4.
[7] *Ibid.*, p. 1.
[8] *Ibid.*, p. 58.
[9] *Canada Year Book*, 1959, p. 421.
[10] Hood and Scott, *Output, Labour and Capital in the Canadian Economy*, p. 196.

Unfortunately the present nationwide system of vital statistics was not established until 1926, and one is driven to a reconstruction of the record through the use of such census and immigration figures as are available, rather as a dinosaur might be reconstructed from a tooth and a tailbone. The method of reconstruction is simple for the population figures. British life tables adjusted to Canadian levels enable one to say what part of the population counted in a given census would be expected to be alive at the date of the next census. The expected figure can be compared with the number actually present, and if it is higher one assumes that the difference is due to net out-migration; if lower, to immigration. Thus the 1861 population numbered 3,230,000 persons of all ages; according to the death rates assumed, the number of survivors of these to 1871 would have been 2,820,000; the actual count of persons ten years of age and over in the 1871 census was 2,630,000; it is supposed, therefore, that the difference, 190,000 persons, was the net migration out of the

TABLE I

A RECONSTRUCTION OF CANADA'S POPULATION RECORD, 1851-1951

(Figures given are in thousands per decade)

	Births	Deaths	Immigration	Emigration (residual)	Population
1851					2,436
	1,281	611	209	86	
1861					3,230
	1,369	718	187	377	
1871					3,689
	1,477	754	353	439	
1881					4,325
	1,538	824	903	1,110	
1891					4,833
	1,546	828	326	505	
1901					5,371
	1,931	811	1,782	1,067	
1911					7,207
	2,338	1,018	1,592	1,330	
1921					8,788
	2,414	1,053	1,195	967	
1931					10,377
	2,291	1,070	150	241	
1941					11,507
	3,205	1,216	548	380	
1951					14,009
TOTALS	19,390	8,903	7,245	6,502	

country. The immigration record shows, however, that 187,000 persons entered during the decade; the total number who left must have been 377,000. Unfortunately, the children under ten years of age who immigrated to Canada are not statistically distinguishable from those who were born here; those who emigrated before they were old enough to be caught in a census left no statistical trace. Minor adjustments of an arbitrary amount were made to fill these gaps.[11]

The resulting figures for the hundred years from 1851 to 1951 are shown in Table I. During the century some 19,400,000 children were born in Canada, and 8,900,000 persons of all ages died, making an addition of 10,500,000 persons by natural increase. The number of immigrants over the whole century was 7,200,000, and of emigrants 6,500,000; the contribution of migration would seem to be only 700,000.

Effect of Immigration

Aside from inaccuracies arising out of the method of calculation, care must be taken in the only interpretation of a statistical table which can be of interest: the imputation of causes. If no migrants had crossed our borders in either direction, our population would be what it now is, less the 700,000 of net immigration shown in the table. But the elimination of all in-migration would have reduced our population by more than this, for not all of the emigrants had earlier been immigrants. Many of the Canadian-born would have emigrated whether or not there had been immigrants. It has been argued that native Canadians who left for the United States did so because of the pressure of immigrants from Europe, but the difference in the occupations of the Europeans who came in and the Canadians who went out makes this seem improbable. Mabel Timlin refers to the "possibility that under some economic conditions the entry of immigrants may have the effect of reducing rather than increasing emigration."[12] The effect of immigration on our population can be underestimated also by forgetting that immigrants who come to Canada, stay a few years, and then leave are subject to natural increase during the time they are here. If we "borrow" a million immigrants for a ten-year period (that is, if we have a million immigrants in one dec-

---

[11] An account of the assumptions and enough arithmetical detail to permit reproduction of the figures from original sources is given in N. Keyfitz, "The Growth of Canadian Population," *Population Studies*, IV (June, 1950), 47-63. An improved calculation has since been worked out by Duncan M. McDougall, *Canadian Journal of Economics and Political Science*, XXVII (May, 1961), 162.
[12] Mabel Timlin, *Does Canada Need More People?* (Oxford, 1951), p. 6.

ade and a million emigrants in the next), then—depending on their age distribution—200,000 or more Canadians will be added to the population. The general point has been well made by Norman Ryder.

Much of this argument has an old-fashioned ring; it goes back to the times when immigration was numerically important in Canada and could shift the balance of religion and language groups. In 1913 immigrants numbered over 400,000 in a population of less than 8,000,000, that is, they were 5 per cent. In our largest year of post-war immigration, 1957, there were 282,000 immigrants coming to a population of 16,589,000, or only 1.7 per cent. The decline of immigration as a political issue must be related to the decline of this percentage.

It would be useful to know more about how the public generally and special groups in Canada feel about immigration. The Canadian Institute of Public Opinion has found out, at different times and in different provinces, how many people are in favour of immigrants and how many are against them. A further step would be to find out from what picture of the Canadian economy and Canadian politics the several shades of sentiment have grown. Getting this picture would take a good deal of interviewing, and there is little of this to report on here, but one can imagine two sorts of popular models which might have some currency in the consciousness of people.

One is that our wealth consists largely of raw materials, and our income is chiefly obtained from their extraction and sale abroad. Those Canadians who do other things—manufacturing, services, etc.—are not really productive, but are only collecting their part of the income from the sale of raw materials, being helped in doing so by tariffs and other devices. On this model the receipts from sales of raw materials abroad are divided among the residents of Canada, after deduction of charges for capital borrowed from foreigners. If the amount of these sales is fixed by limitations of either natural resources or foreign markets, then the fewer Canadians above the number needed for the work of extraction the higher the per capita income.

But when, on the other hand, the Canadian economy comes to be seen as indefinitely expansible because based on local manufacturing production which is genuinely valuable, and the newcomers are viewed as both producers and the market for production, the limitations of land, raw materials, and foreign markets tend to be given a minor place. While conservation of resources is still important, the long-term Malthusian elements in the argument tend to be replaced by such organizational matters as bringing the immigrants in during the spring so as to minimize winter unemployment. Herbert Marshall's notion of absorptive capacity is broken down by Mabel Timlin into short and long-term elements, the former including the training and finding of jobs for the immigrants. In a social security minded age these short-term elements are not unimportant.

The models of our economy and national life implicit in popular views regarding the desirability of immigration are blended with other items which might be called political—especially the relative strength of religious and other groups. For a considerable period of time Gallup poll surveys showed less enthusiasm for immigration on the part of trade union members and French-speaking citizens than on the part of employers and English-speaking citizens. It would be worth finding more about the configuration of outlook of members of these groups, especially what mental calculations they make of the impact their group would have on national life if it came to dominate.

Some change in such thinking undoubtedly takes place through time. As we get further from dependence on nature for our support, the number of population that could physically establish and feed themselves becomes less important, and the way in which they will affect our social and economic organization correspondingly more important. Between the time of Griffith Taylor and that of Mabel Timlin there lies not only a vast increase in sophistication about how society works, but also an objective change in the way in which Canadians make their living. If there is any reappearance of the notion of dependence on raw materials, it tends to take the form that our resources are greater than those of the United States and so justify greater immigration. As has happened throughout our history, those moments when our resources become a focus of interest for the outside world bring capital and people simultaneously across our borders.

One of the ways in which the immigration of the present time differs from that of a generation ago is in the proportion of migrants who stay in the country. This is seen by considering the immigrants of 1946-51, for instance, and comparing the number who entered in those years with the number among them caught in the census; the proportion was 80 per cent. The corresponding figure for 1926-31, the last occasion when a census followed on a burst of immigration, was 64 per cent. One would like to be able to say that the greater retention is in some measure a contemporary Canadian achievement;

unfortunately, however, we have no data on the effect of the tightening of United States immigration policy on the Canadian situation.

Deaths

We dispose first of the negative element in natural increase—deaths. The downward trend of the death rate is not striking in the over-all figures of male deaths per thousand population, which were 10.5 in 1931 and 9.5 in 1957. For females, the decline is considerably more rapid—from 9.6 to 6.9 per thousand over the same period. It is in particular age-sex groups that the most striking improvements are shown: from 96 to 34 deaths under one year of age per thousand boys born in the period 1931 to 1957; from 3.8 down to .9 deaths per thousand women aged twenty-five to twenty-nine years. As one goes up the scale of ages the trends become less and less distinct; at ages over fifty for males and over eighty for women the improvements become negligible. These changes are, of course, the reflections of success in attacking particular causes of death: deaths caused by tuberculosis fell from about 75 per 100,000 to 7, those associated with childbirth from 10.7 to 1.5; at the same time deaths from heart disease, cancer, and motor vehicle accidents went up.

All this is seen in an increase of the expectation of life for men at age zero from 60.00 years to 67.61 years between 1931 and 1956; for women the increase was even more striking: from 62.10 to 72.92 years. The expectation at birth has increased at the rate of three years per decade for men, four years per decade for women. However, there is no tangible evidence that this can be continued; existing achievements have reached their limit since at the ages to which they apply the death rate has dropped nearly to zero. From 1931 to 1956, the expectation of life at age forty-five improved hardly at all for men, and for women only three years. The present stage seems to be one of diminishing returns on the application of medicine: as we are saved from one ill we succumb quickly to another. On this reading of the figures any further dramatic fall in the death rate must depend on a direct attack on old age itself.

The possibility of some altogether new means of prolonging life crops up in the news from time to time. Science which has probed outer space and harnessed the atom may not take many more years to find out how to prevent the modification of the body cells which constitutes aging. This opens out for forward-looking citizens the perhaps exhilarating prospect of living for centuries. We would escape from the present uneconomic system by which out of a life of seventy-five years the first twenty or twenty-five are spent in education or preparation and the last ten in retirement. Not the least of the benefits might be a new sense of responsibility among statesmen who will themselves have to face the future that their political actions bring about.

The Falling Birth Rate

Crude birth rates may be calculated for the hundred-year period from Table I. If births averaged 128,100 for the ten years 1851-61 and the average population (worked out by adding that at the beginning to that at the end of the decade and dividing by 2) was 2,833,000 persons, then the ten years averaged 45 births per thousand population. From this time there is a remarkably steady decline decade by decade down to the low in 1931-41 of 21 per thousand.

It is not surprising that during those years the downward trend of the birth rate became fixed as inevitable in the minds of everyone who wrote about the matter. Canada seemed to be sharing with the whole of the Western world a declining willingness to reproduce itself. Philosophical writers assumed that the decline had deep causes, that it was symptomatic of the declining morale of Western civilization. Where not long before a book by E. A. Ross with the title *Standing Room Only* had been widely read, now Enid Charles' *The Twilight of Parenthood* seemed the best heading under which to analyse the trend. Vast moral, economic, political, and social conclusions were drawn from the statistical material.

The conclusions drawn in the early 1930's by scholars Burton Hurd and M. C. MacLean on the future population of Canada were a projection of this trend into the future. They found that the "ultimate" population of Canada was shaping up to about 13 millions; this figure would be reached by about 1960 and would be followed by a decline. We could not exceed this ultimate total unless, like the later Roman Empire, we invited within our borders the vigorous barbarians of those parts of the world that had not yet been touched by our decadence.

It appeared that the decay began and had its most serious manifestations in the upper classes. Those who had most benefited from the wealth and education that the community had to offer were those who most sharply limited their families. The cities especially, in which were found both the best and the worst that civilization had produced, were not replenishing their populations. About the best that could be hoped for was that the country-side would retain its vigour and that its fresh sons and daughters would maintain the necessary complement of the cities. But this brought a new concern into the minds of students of population: the danger that the stock was running down. This followed logically from the assumptions that the wealthier and better educated people were the better stock, and that the qualities that made them so were hereditary. The progressive deterioration of the race was even measured; in England Sir Cyril Burt found that intelligence was running down by one or two I.Q. points per generation.[13] Even those who laughed at such arguments feared that the people who were reproducing themselves would transmit their inferiority to their children through nurture if not through nature.

In few fields of scholarly endeavour can the outlook have changed so completely in one generation from that portrayed above. We can now see a longer period of history and realize that over thousands of years the birth and death rates have been very nearly equal; that it was inevitable that the sudden decline in the death rate of the nineteenth century be followed by a decline in the birth rate; that like many social changes this was initiated by the most sensitive elements of the population—the educated, the wealthy, the urban— but that the differential birth rate would not continue indefinitely, any more than would the decline in the birth rate. The differential was a cross-section of the process of adjustment to the lower level now needed for reproduction. The rise of the birth rate over the last twenty years suggests a totally different interpretation of the preceding decline.

The Passing of the Differential Birth Rate

The most important thing that can be said about the Canadian birth rate of this generation is that its differentials are rapidly disappearing. One may start to look into this by comparing provinces. In 1921, the birth rate in Quebec was 37.6 and in Ontario 25.3. By 1956 Quebec's rate had declined to 29.4, a drop of 21.8 per cent, while Ontario's rate had risen to 26.6. Whereas the nine provinces ranged from as low as 20 to as high as 38 in 1921, the variation by 1956 was between a low of 26 and a high of 31 (excluding Newfoundland at

[13] "The Trend of National Intelligence," *British Journal of Sociology*, I (June 1950), 154-68.

both dates). In the course of thirty-five years, a situation in which the highest province was nearly double the lowest gave place to one in which the highest was only 19.2 per cent above the lowest. This reduction in the dispersion suggests some considerable changes, despite the fact that the average for Canada over the thirty-five years only dropped from 29.3 to 28.0.

One would like to know if this approach to uniformity applies among income classes. Unfortunately, income is not given on the birth certificate, and even if it were it would be difficult to relate it to income of the population as a whole and so establish rates by income. But the family tables of the successive censuses show both number of resident children and wage income. We consider only the censuses of 1941 and 1951, and confine the comparison to families whose head is from thirty-five to forty-four years of age.

In 1951, the average number of children under fourteen years of age in those families whose head was a wage-earner earning $1,000-$1,499 was 2.22, while in those where the earnings were $4,000-$5,999 the average was 1.69. If we take it that these 1951 income classes correspond to $450-$949 and $1,950-$2,949 in 1941, then the corresponding pair of figures for children under fifteen years of age is 2.27 and 1.62. Having to compare children under fourteen with those under fifteen is regrettable, and the comparison of money incomes is unreliable, but the convergence is nevertheless clear.

Similarly for education; here inflation does not enter in to confuse the 1941 and 1951 comparisons. Again, we consider family heads of thirty-five to forty-four years, and are forced to compare those under fourteen in normal families in 1951 with those under fifteen in all families in 1941. The contrast which should bring out the result most clearly is that between heads with one to four years of schooling and those with thirteen or more years. Averages are 2.88 against 1.61 for 1941 and 2.80 against 1.74 for 1951, an even sharper closing of the differential than appeared for income.

It is possible also to compare the trend in family size of those of French origin with those of British origin. Confining ourselves to families of which the head is in the above mentioned age group, considering only children under six years of age, and starting in the province of Quebec, we find for French origin a drop from 1.44 in 1941 to 1.19 in 1951, and for British origin a rise from .74 to .77. The same contrast is shown in the province of Ontario where the French showed a drop from 1.22 to .98 and the British stood at .68 in both years. These differences are in effect a comparison of births between

1935 and 1941, on the one hand, and between 1945 and 1951 on the other.

The rural and urban statistics tell a similar story. These census categories have an administrative and historical character, and there can be no pretence that they are statistically homogeneous from one date to another. But they serve our purpose to the extent that census urban has on the average a somewhat more urban character than does census rural. Unfortunately, the 1951 census tabulations for Canada do not make the distinction between rural and urban families according to age of head, but tabulations were made for the Maritime provinces. In the Maritime thirty-five to forty-four age group, we find that the 1941 figures are 2.14 children under age fifteen per family in urban parts and 2.89 in rural. In 1951, the corresponding figures (except that they are given for children under age fourteen) are 2.04 and 2.29. Thus the rural was 35 per cent higher than the urban in 1941 and 12 per cent higher in 1951.

However, it is not only city life and the direct effect on family size of its rational consciousness with which we need be concerned. For in the country-side there are differences as well. The people who live nearer to the city have the smaller families; those farther away are less affected. In any attempt to document this point it is necessary to hold constant income, education, and occupation. This was done for a sample of farm families from the 1941 census, in which the comparison was made of the number of children ever born to women forty-five years of age and over. Holding constant some sixteen extraneous variables, it turned out that the French Catholic families far from cities in Quebec were larger by 1.28 children on the average than the French Catholic families near cities, and in Ontario, comparing English Protestant families, the difference was .70 children in favour of the distant families.[14]

The Change in Ages of Mothers

Changes also have taken place in the ages at which women have children. In the period from 1931 to 1954 the proportion of children born to mothers in their twenties has increased from 53 per cent to over 57 per cent, and the number of children born to mothers over forty has declined from 6.2 per cent to 3.9 per cent. The average age of both mothers and fathers at the time of birth of their children has

[14]N. Keyfitz, "Differential Fertility in Ontario: An Application of Factorial Design to a Demographic Problem," *Population Studies*, VI (Nov., 1952).

declined: mothers averaged 29.2 years in 1931 and 28.4 years in 1954. Age specific birth rates are available for five-year groups since 1921. It turns out that women aged twenty to twenty-four have shown about a 50 per cent increase between 1921-5 and 1957, from 150 children per thousand women to 226. Age twenty-five to twenty-nine years shows a 25 per cent increase, from 176 to 225. Age thirty to thirty-four shows little net change over the period while ages from thirty-five onward show a substantial decline. Younger ages at marriage are a part of what is reflected in these figures; the fall seems to be about one year of age per decade for grooms and three-quarters of a year for brides.

It has always been true that the vast majority of first and second births occurred among women under thirty years of age. Might the preceding data be associated with more first and second births and fewer higher order births in proportion to the total? The point is important for the future; if an increase occurs in total births due entirely to an increase in first births, then it might well be the result of a just-preceding increase in marriages, and in any case no such increase in first births alone could do much for long-run fertility. The comparison by birth order has been made over the twenty-year period from 1927-33 to 1947-53, and it turns out that the increases are confined to the first three orders of birth.[15] It is second births which have increased most sharply—by almost 40 per cent; third and first births increased between 20 per cent and 30 per cent; fourth and later births declined more and more with increasing order, so that ninth births showed a decline of almost 60 per cent. Of course data of this kind ought to be related to the number of women capable of having third births for example (as the actuaries say, "exposed to risk"), that is, women who have had second births. Shifts in the numbers exposed would obviously affect the interpretation of the figures above, but the subject is too big to be taken up here. The work of Norman Ryder has contributed importantly to our knowledge in this field.

To account for these results would be a large task, but there is no doubt that they are associated with the growth of cities and especially of suburbs. Seeley, Sim, and Loosley discuss this with penetration. "Many women, alone with their children and their labour-saving gadgets, long for the day when, the children in school, they may again go out to 'join in the life of the community' "; which is to say,

[15] Later data would show that the increases have moved into higher orders of birth and a few more years may show it moving higher still.

when they may take a job once more. But not all the women of Crestwood Heights took this view: "At the opposite pole are the women who continue to make home and children the centre of existence. Some of these may be literally forced out unwillingly into the community when the children are grown and they suddenly find themselves emotionally bankrupt in an empty house."[16]

Urban and Suburban Growth

The census figures are arranged conveniently for the student who wishes to distinguish population growth within the large cities from growth in the areas around them. Between 1951 and 1956 the incorporated city of Montreal increased by 88,000 persons or 9 per cent, while the municipalities contiguous to it increased by 137,000 persons or 37 per cent. This continued the changes of the period 1941-51 when the city proper increased by 13 per cent and the fringe areas by 58 per cent.

The contrast for Toronto is greater yet; while during the fifteen-year period the city proper showed a negligible change, the fringe areas multiplied threefold (from 242,000 persons in 1941 to 690,000 in 1956) by which time they had outstripped the central city. Toronto also shows an age selection in the settlement of the suburbs. The ratio of children under fifteen years of age to the population was 29 per cent in the suburbs as compared with 20 per cent in the city proper. At the other extreme of life, 11 per cent of the city population is sixty-five years of age and over, as against 6 per cent of the fringe areas.

These figures are not surprising. The city is bound to fill up before population spreads beyond it. New York shows this in its several boroughs: Manhattan reached its peak in 1910 and has since fallen by 25 per cent; Brooklyn and the Bronx reached their peaks in 1950; Queens is still growing. That Montreal shows this effect less than Toronto is owing partly to its greater area (50 square miles as compared with 35), partly to its including such areas as Outremont, Westmount, and Verdun, and partly also to the fact that Montrealers are less insistent on individual houses than are Torontonians. Nor is it surprising that people with young children take to the suburbs while those whose families are grown wish to return to the city.

[16] J. R. Seeley, R. A. Sim, and Elizabeth Loosley, *Crestwood Heights: A North American Suburb* (Toronto, 1956), p. 180.

Conclusion

An attempt has here been made to discern some of the main trends in Canadian population growth and to say something about the circumstances under which these are developing. Prominent among current trends is a rise in the birth rate after more than a half century of decline. More important than this rise in the average is the convergence of rates for the several groups; the urban, educated, prosperous, English-speaking families are increasing, the rural, less educated, poorer, French-speaking families decreasing. People are leaving the country-side to take urban jobs; they are also leaving the cities and going out to the suburbs. The suburbs are made up of individually owned homes and are made possible by the administration of the mortgage market.

It is an aspect of the difficulty of imputing causes—without which social science is lame indeed—that we cannot say in what degree people build houses in the suburbs because they have children who do not fit into city apartments, and to what extent they have children once they get to the suburbs to fill the rooms of their new houses. To the extent that the latter is the direction of motivation, the availability of mortgage funds could be said to be a cause of our birth rate which is now almost unique. Britain, France, and other Western European countries showed a rise in the birth rate after the war, but they have now fallen back almost to pre-war levels. The United States, with 25 births per thousand population, nearly equals Canada. Says Conrad Taeuber of the United States:

In our case the range of child-woman ratios among Divisions in 1920 was 70 per cent, and by 1950 it had dropped to 40 per cent. The observations that differentials by income, occupation, and education have been narrowing could also be followed through in United States materials. There is some indication that differentials between white and Negro have been narrowing as well, as there apparently has between the major ethnic groups in the Canadian population.

And to carry the comparison a step further, the decline in higher order births at the same time that the birth rate has shown some increase is one more of the developments which indicate the similarity of the underlying conditions.[17]

Dr. Taeuber argues that the main difference between Canada and the United States—our family allowances—is therefore not the cause of our high birth rate. The similarity, in which both Canada and the United States contrast with Europe, is in the degree of prosperity and availability of housing.

[17] Comments, Meeting of the Population Association of America, Chicago, May 3-4, 1958.

Projections of future population have inevitably been determined not only by the levels of birth and death at the times when they were calculated, but also by the moods of optimism or pessimism which prevailed at that time. I have mentioned above the estimates of Burton W. Hurd and M. C. MacLean in the early 1930's that within two or three decades of when they wrote Canada would exhaust its possibilities of expansion, and that its population would decline from a maximum of about 13 million. Somewhat later Enid Charles was more optimistic. Using Notestein's method she found that by 1971 the population would be 14 to 14.5 million, an increase of only half a million during the decade 1961-71.[18] Successive projections have gradually raised the future figure; the most recent and apparently the most careful and realistic are those of Hood and Scott who find for 1980 some 26,653,000 residents of Canada on their median assumption of a net balance of immigration of 75,000 persons per year.

We can visualize this considerable population, two-thirds of it living in urban places if present trends continue, but spreading out over suburban fringes, with better and better health, deaths down to the point where nearly everyone lives to an age of seventy, and families determined at between two and four children each.

[18] *The Changing Size of the Family in Canada* (Dominion Bureau of Statistics, 1948), p. 28.

The Suburban Community[1]

S. D. CLARK

"I SPEAK in this paper," David Riesman wrote, in the opening sentence of an article entitled "The Suburban Sadness," "from the perspective of one who loves city and country, but not the suburbs."[2] Riesman is not alone in his dislike of the suburbs, if one can judge the prevalence of a state of feeling by the tenor of the kind of articles which find a prominent place in popular journals or of books which publishers feel are sufficiently saleable to justify paperbacks concerned with the suburban way of life.[3] It has become fashionable to say unkind things about the suburbs as, fifty years ago, it was fashionable to say unkind things about the city. Then the city, pictured in all its depravity, corruption, and shallowness, was set over against a romantic image of the country to bring into pleasant relief the simplicity, warm-heartedness, and virtuousness of the rural way of life. In the past fifty years, the Riesmans have learned to love the city in the manner that they love the country, and now it is "suburbia," portrayed in terms of a stupid conformity, fetish of togetherness, and craze for organization which is set over against a romantic image of the city with a way of life giving expression to such qualities of man as self-reliance, discriminating judgment, and sturdy independence.

Not everything written about the suburban community has been in the vein of either holding up to ridicule the suburban way of life

[1] I am indebted to Central Mortgage and Housing Corporation for a grant which made possible the carrying out of a study of the Toronto suburban community. While some of the findings of this study are suggested here, there is no attempt to present the data on which the findings are based. This is undertaken in a larger study, soon, I hope, to be published. It is scarcely necessary to say that Central Mortgage and Housing Corporation is in no way responsible for the views expressed. The greatest possible freedom was accorded by the Corporation in the carrying on of the study.

[2] William M. Dobriner, ed., *The Suburban Community* (New York, 1958), pp. 375-408.

[3] Of books, William H. Whyte, Jr., *The Organization Man* (New York, 1956) is the one which has attracted the most attention; Part VII is devoted to suburbia. John Keats, *The Crack in the Picture Window* (New York, 1957) and A. C. Spectorsky, *The Exurbanites* (New York, 1955) are further examples. It would serve no useful purpose to attempt to list the very great number of articles on suburbia appearing in popular and semi-popular journals and magazines.

or seeing in this way of life a threat to the most cherished of our social values. The problem of suburban development has attracted the attention of a number of serious students of society.[4] So deeply imbedded, however, in the thinking about suburbanism is the kind of bias given expression by Riesman that it cannot be dismissed as characteristic only of those writers seeking to make a popular appeal. Students of suburbia have gone from reading Riesman to reading Fromm and Whyte, and to a picture of a suburban society producing a population of "other-directed" men has been added a picture of a society caught up in a system of bureaucratic organization and mass communication, producing through the exaction of a rigorous conformity a population of either neurotics or "organization men."[5]

By concentrating attention upon certain kinds of suburban areas, it has not been difficult to build up such an image of suburban society or, indeed, of a suburban personality type. Thus, for instance, from the picture presented in *Crestwood Heights*[6] of what is reputed to be a North American suburb, much could be made of the kind of social pressures characteristic of suburban life. Had those who have thus used the *Crestwood Heights* study, however, known Toronto better, known something about the hundreds of subdivisions spreading east to Whitby, north to Newmarket, and west to Brampton and beyond, known even more that Forest Hill Village at the time it was being studied was two generations old, they would have realized how little typical of a suburban community this community was, if, indeed, it could in any sense be considered suburban at all.[7] Back in the 1920's, Burgess discovered his famous concentric

[4] This paper was written before I had an opportunity to read Bennet M. Berger, *Working-Class Suburb* (Berkeley and Los Angeles, 1960). In this study of a suburban community made up of auto workers, Berger does a masterful job of exposing "the myth of suburbia." His findings agree almost completely with mine. Berger, however, gives emphasis to the negative aspects of suburban life. What he is concerned in showing is that the way of life of the population he studied grows out of its working-class culture and not out of its suburban situation, and in this he is quite right. What I argue in this paper is that there is a difference, however, between the suburban and the urban society, but the difference is to be accounted for simply on the grounds that the suburban society is new. This aspect of the problem is not developed by Berger but to the extent that he does touch on it he says nothing with which I would not agree.

Though Robert C. Wood, in *Surburbia: Its People and Their Politics* (Boston, 1959), relies heavily upon what have been accepted as studies of typical suburban communities, the liveliness of the thesis developed justifies its special mention.

[5] See, besides Whyte, *The Organization Man*, Erich Fromm, *The Sane Society* (London, 1956).

[6] J. R. Seeley, R. A. Sim, and E. W. Loosley, *Crestwood Heights: A North American Suburb* (Toronto, 1956).

[7] For the student of local government, the classification of all those areas lying outside the incorporated limits of the city as suburban may serve a useful purpose. For sociol-

circles, zones of development spreading out from the centre of the city, the outermost zone which he labelled "surburban." This was the zone of well-to-do residential development: in the Toronto area, the Forest Hill villages of the 1920-1930's, the Don Mills and Thorncrest villages of the 1940-1950's. Somehow, this notion that the suburban community is a community of the rich or of those who hope to become rich has hardened in much of the thinking and writing about suburbanism.

It is not too hard to understand why this was the case. In the first phase of urban growth, it is only the well-to-do who can afford to live miles outside the city and still enjoy urban services. The provision of such services lies beyond the financial capacity of municipalities largely rural in population and they must thus be provided by the residents themselves. On the other hand, the great stretches of open country-side make possible the kind of experiments in community building, free from the encroachments of the city, which people of means can afford to undertake. Thus develop the smart, new, planned residential areas of the suburbs, housing a population typically upper middle class in character, rising young business executives, professional people, and the like.

The isolation of such residential areas from the built-up areas of the urban community, their physical compactness, and their development around a well-defined centre make them easy to study. They have clear-cut boundaries and there is an orderliness in the structure of their social life. They do appear to have some sort of ethos or character and they do appear to encourage a distinctive personality type. Such can scarcely fail to be the case in view of the fact that it is only certain kinds of people which settle in them.

To what extent the description which emerges of the suburban society is really a description of a particular urban class (and perhaps as well ethnic grouping) is a question which need not be gone into here. What does have to be asked, however, whatever may be

ogy, however, such a definition of suburban is meaningless. Otherwise, areas like Leaside, Long Branch, and York Township outside Toronto will have to be considered suburban for years to come if they maintain their separate corporate existence. Particularly misleading in this respect is the census division between the city and metropolitan area. The census figures may not give Toronto and Montreal a larger suburban population than they really have since suburban areas actually extend far beyond metropolitan limits, but the population of what must be considered the *urban community* is much larger than the census figures suggest. On the other hand, by the use of these figures, one would conclude that Edmonton and Calgary had no suburbs; all the growth has taken place within the corporate limits. At the time of the *Crestwood Heights* study not only was the population of Forest Hill Village two generations old but it had changed very substantially in ethnic composition.

the character of the society which develops in these planned residential areas, is the question of how representative this society is of suburban society in general. The Whytes and others who have written about "suburbia" have too often been taken to be writing about the typical suburban community, and may even have encouraged this conclusion. Yet nowhere in the literature on suburbia is there a recognition of the simple fact that of the great number of people who move out of the city into the surrounding country-side during a period of rapid urban growth only a very small fraction move into those kinds of residential areas which have been subjected to investigation and analysis.

Within the dimensions of a paper such as this it is clearly not possible to examine all the different kinds of movements of population from the city to the suburbs which take place as a result of urban growth. In general terms, however, two fairly distinct phases of development can be distinguished. The first phase involves the establishment of the kind of residential areas Whyte and others have written about. But it involves as well two other very different kinds of development, one characterized by the movement of people of moderate means into the suburbs, a second by the movement of people in impoverished circumstances. Both of these developments have been almost wholly ignored by the student of suburbia. For this he might be forgiven. Not so easy to forgive, however, is his neglect of that phase of development which follows the first, characterized by the mass movement of population into the suburbs. It is this mass movement which creates the suburban community as we know it. Yet in the literature on suburbia it receives virtually no attention.

To an examination of the nature of this later phase of suburban development most of this paper will be devoted. It is in the character of the society growing out of the mass movement of population into the suburbs that is to be found an understanding of the phenomenon of suburbanism. Before turning to such an examination, however, some attention must be given to those other types of suburban development taking place at the same time as the development of planned residential areas, the one involving the movement of people of moderate means into the suburbs, the other the movement of people in impoverished circumstances. Out of this earlier phase of development grow the forces leading to the later phase of the mass movement of population to the suburbs.

In the early phase of urban growth, not only the rich or near rich but persons of moderate means, by taking advantage of transportation links with the city provided by already existing roads, and of lot or house prices determined by prevailing farm or village property values, can afford to move out into the country providing only that they do not arrive in such numbers in any particular rural or village area as to impose an intolerable burden upon established municipal services (or drive up to speculative levels lot and house prices). Thus occurs that ribbon kind of development, long the despair of the community planner, characterized by the spreading out of urban residents into areas far distant from the city and the creating of a society which, though neither rural nor urban, is one which possesses some of the qualities of both. It would be difficult, indeed, to fit this society into any kind of stereotype of suburbia. There is here no distinctive pattern of social relationships; no distinctive personality type. Yet, in terms of the number of people involved, this kind of development must clearly be taken into account in seeking an understanding of the way in which the city extends itself into the country.[8]

Equally important is the other kind of development taking place during this early phase of urban growth beyond established city boundaries. This is the spread of impoverished sections of the urban population out of the crowded downtown areas of the city into the country. That this development takes place almost completely unnoticed can be accounted for by the fact that the areas selected for settlement ordinarily lie back out of sight from the main arteries of travel and are far distant from the city. The man of moderate means who is prepared to forego city services in moving to the country is influenced by two considerations in deciding upon a place to reside: the price of land and transportation to the city. In the case of the very poor, the price of land becomes such a dominant consideration that little regard can be paid to transportation. Settlement thus tends to take place along back country roads or in those hidden pockets of marginal farm land where once summer colonies may have grown up or where, if no previous development has taken place, residential lots are sold off at prices much less than commanded by land suitable for agricultural purposes. Where extensive stretches of such marginal farm land are to be found, there may develop large heavily populated residential areas made up of row upon row of cheaply

[8] This kind of development has, of course, attracted a good deal of attention of urban ecologists and of sociologists interested in its impact on small town society. Spectorsky's *The Exurbanites*, however, can hardly be considered an adequate examination of this development.

constructed frame cottages, set upon wooden posts, lacking inside plumbing, running water, or any form of central heating. In the whole peripheral area surrounding the large city, the number of people moving into areas such as these may run into several thousand. Such certainly is the case in the Toronto area. For lack of a better word, this might be called a cottage type of development.

Thus for every planned residential area of the Don Mills or Thorncrest Village type which is created by the spread out from the city of people of above average income, there develop these other very different kinds of residential areas accommodating people whose incomes range down from what might be considered average to considerably below.[9] In all probability, in terms of the number of people involved, these latter developments considerably outweigh the former in importance. The city, in terms of all its population types, seeks in effect to reproduce itself in the country.

But this it can do only to a degree so long as certain conditions persist which place a sharp limit upon urban growth. This is a phase of selective growth. Not every one at this point in the growth of the city is tempted to move into the suburbs. Indeed, for the vast majority of persons seeking residential accommodation during this early phase of development the suburbs have little to offer.[10] These are persons who cannot afford a home in the planned residential areas growing up in the country, while for such persons a home built along a country highway or on the outskirts of a country village has little appeal. On the other hand, the plight of such people is not sufficiently desperate to prompt their location in one of those sub-

[9] Not all of the residential developments of the first type, it should be pointed out, are made up of people of above average income. The development may be one resulting from the co-operative efforts of a group of working-class people, for instance, or it may be sponsored by an industrial firm which has moved out from the city and brought its workers with it. A better way of describing these developments might be to call them collectively sponsored. Bathurst Manor in the township of North York should certainly be considered a development similar in character to Don Mills and Thorncrest Village, though planning here was less in evidence. For the purposes of this paper, it seemed better to confine attention largely to the Don Mills and Thorncrest Village planned type of development and exclude consideration of those other types of development which, without much planning, achieved the same character of homogeneity because of a strong ethnic or social class basis of selection.

Similarly, the discussion here of the ribbon type of development and of that type involving the movement of impoverished sections of the urban population into country areas far distant from the city suggests distinctions more clear-cut than they are in reality. But at the polar extremes there are vast differences between these two types of development, and between them and the planned type.

[10] That is to say, the "new suburbs." In the Toronto area, in the years immediately before and after World War II, there was a great deal of filling in of residential areas which had developed during the boom period of the 1920's, Leaside, for example.

standard or cottage-type residential communities growing up far distant from the city. Thus suburban growth during this phase of development is characterized by what appears as a sort of haphazard occupation of country areas, the differential price of land and the availability of certain public services, and in particular of roads leading into the city, determining the over-all pattern of growth. In this manner occurred the settlement, in the Toronto area, of the townships of Etobicoke, North York, and Scarborough in the years 1945-53 and in this manner is occurring the settlement of certain more distant townships today. Where development is of this haphazard sort, the establishment of the planned residential community in the suburbs (the Don Mills or Thorncrest Villages of the 1945-53 period) can scarcely fail to command attention.

However, the whole of the growth of the urban community outwards during this early phase of development is of insignificant proportions when compared with the growth which comes after. Here and there, a Thorncrest Village or Don Mills becomes established; further out, along highways reaching into the country, a scattering of urban families take up residence in areas that are still basically rural in character; and still more distant, hidden from public view, spring up those clusterings of cheaply constructed if picturesque cottage homes housing a population drawn from the city's most impoverished social classes. But vast stretches of open country-side yet remain to be occupied. Their occupation can come only with a type of development very different from that of this early phase.

Yet it is this earlier phase of development which creates the conditions for the later. The mass movement of population into the suburbs comes only with the production of the kind of housing that reaches a mass market and before there is such production the occupation of the country-side surrounding the city must reach the point where a certain level of services of an urban character can be supported. Once this "break through" point is reached, however, there is virtually no limit to the residential growth that can take place, and private enterprise, in the mass assembly of land and mass building of homes, is not slow to take advantage of the opportunity thus opened up to reach a suddenly vastly widened housing market. In the early phase of suburban development, the economies of settlement depend upon the limitation of the occupation of any particular area to the point where the burden imposed on long established public services can be borne, except where, as in the planned type of residential development, the occupation involves the establishment of such services by the residents themselves. In this later phase of development, however, the economies of settlement are such that what becomes of crucial importance is the full occupation of the newly serviced areas in the shortest possible time. The movement of population into the suburbs as a result now takes on the character of a great rushing wave sweeping all before it. Thus were the townships of Etobicoke, North York, and Scarborough occupied in the years 1953-57, and so are some of the townships lying beyond being occupied today.[11]

What requires emphasis with respect to this development is its non-selective character in terms of the kind of people involved. There occurs here what is truly a mass movement of population. Among the people settling in the suburbs can be found still many well-to-do and many very poor, and, settling along country roads ever more distant from the city, are those families prepared to sacrifice urban services for the advantages of country life. But overrunning the vast country-side are people of much less distinctive type, the great house-hungry population of the city which can find space for itself only by spreading beyond the limits of the urban community.

If there is a suburban society, the people settling in these mass-produced housing areas are its creators. But the society thus created is clearly one which does not conform to any stereotype of suburbia. It has no form; indeed, has no boundaries which can be determined. It cannot be studied in the way that the society of a Don Mills or Thorncrest Village can. It consists of nothing more than a great, undifferentiated mass of dwellings, street blocks, and subdivisions, beginning and ending nowhere that can be seen clearly. And the popu-

[11] The census figures show very well what was happening, for instance, in the township of Scarborough in the years 1951-56. In 1951, 81.2 per cent of the township's population was concentrated in an area south of a jagged line extending eastward along Eglinton Avenue to Midland Avenue and then dropping down to the C.N.R. mainline and following it eastward to Highland Creek and from there down to the lake. Some of this area had been built up in the 1920's and even earlier. In the years 1951-56 that area extending north of Eglinton Avenue and east to Brimley Road, not including the Village of Agincourt, grew from a population of 4,025 to one of 47,641. The smaller triangular area in the centre of the township, bounded by the C.N.R. mainline, Brimley Road, and Eglinton Avenue, grew in the same years from a population of 934 to one of 5,157. The 1961 census will clearly show what, in fact, is now the case that, apart from the northeastern corner, the whole of the township has become fully developed residentially. Indeed, extensive apartment house building in the southwestern corner of the township in recent years indicates the ushering in here of a still later phase of urban growth.

There is no end of examples of subdivision developments which illustrate the pattern of growth in particular areas. In East Gwillimbury Heights outside the town of Newmarket, for instance, the first houses were ready for occupancy in the mid-winter of 1957-58. By the late autumn of 1958 virtually all of the approximately 500 homes in this subdivision were occupied.

lation which inhabits these residential areas stretching out from the city is as little differentiated as the areas themselves. People choose to live in a Don Mills or Thorncrest Village; what they seek is a particular way of life which planned residential areas such as these appear to offer. But for those people who move into the mass-produced housing areas growing up outside the city there is no choice. What they seek is a house and they move where they do only because it is there they can find a house they can afford. This is as true of the person buying a $20,000 house as it is of the person buying a $12,000 house.[12] Though there is a differentiation of residential areas in terms of price, and of population in terms of income, such a differentiation has little or no social significance. The individual choice that is made is on the basis of capacity to pay. What is being bought is a house, not a social environment, and it is this which gives the housing market which grows up under conditions of large-scale residential development the character of a mass market.

It is the failure to see the rise of planned residential areas in the perspective of this much more extensive kind of development involving the production of housing for a mass market which accounts, in the literature on suburbia, for much of the nonsense which has been written. What the student of suburbia has been primarily concerned with is the finding of some sort of order in the phenomenon of suburbanism, and in looking for order he has concentrated attention upon those kinds of suburban areas where a sense of order is most prominent. What he has failed to recognize is that suburbanism is not only an order but a process and that an understanding of suburbanism as a process involves looking at those areas not where a sense of order is the most prominent feature but where it is the least. It is in these latter kinds of areas that are to be discovered the dynamics of suburban growth. There is a pattern of development but it is one in the direction away from order to disorder. This is in the nature of the case where what really is being talked about is a phenomenon of social change. There is nothing about the way suburban society develops different from the way other societies develop.

Indeed, if the pattern of settlement of an area like Western Canada

---

[12] But not of the person buying a $30,000 house. Houses in this price range are not built for a mass market and they are not built except in those areas where there has been sufficient planning to protect property values. Thus persons buying such houses become selected in terms of social class; what they are buying is a social environment as well as a house and they are prepared to pay $30,000 or more for it. Precisely where the line should be drawn between these two different kinds of market is, of course, not easy to determine.

is examined, there will appear a striking similarity between it and the pattern of settlement of the suburban community. Western Canada had its pioneers, families moving far beyond settled areas to wait, perhaps for years, before the surrounding region became occupied and a form of community life developed. It had its experiments in community building, its "backland utopias" created out of the dreams of the visionary or out of the determination of certain people (often of a particular religious faith or ethnic attachment) to preserve a certain way of life; and it had its half-hidden settlements of the impoverished, the economic cast-offs of older societies (though not as many perhaps as did Nova Scotia and Upper Canada much earlier). It was these types of settlements that characterized the early development of Western Canada. But the real occupation of the West came only when this selective type of settlement gave way to the mass movement of land-hungry peoples from Eastern Canada, the United States, and Europe. To have sought for the typical "Westerner" among the people making up one or other of these little ethnic, religious, or other such colonies scattered over the Prairies in the early years of settlement, among, for instance, the people belonging to the little Jewish colony in South-eastern Saskatchewan, would have been as much justified as the search for the typical "suburbanite" among the people taking part in one or other of those planned experiments in community building characteristic, along with the ribbon and cottage type of residential development, of the early phase of suburban growth.

This is not to say that the population moving into the mass-produced housing areas outside the city has no distinctive characteristics. For one thing, it is a population which is very young.[13] For another, it is a population with no previous experience of home

Age	Thorncrest Village (percentage)	Regency Acres (percentage)
25 or less	3	21
26-30	15	31
31-35	21	22
36-40	21	14
40 and up	40	12

[13] In contrast not only to the population of the city but to the population involved in the earlier phase of residential development. The contrast to the population of the city is striking.

ownership.[14] It is a population which has used up all its savings in the purchase of a home and its furnishing. It can well be described as a foot-loose population. The typical pattern of movement has been from a flat after marriage, to an apartment, to a house in the suburbs. There has been here no identification with a particular way of life, no putting down of roots in a particular community. Before the purchase of the house, the total investment has been in marriage and the founding of a family.

A population such as this does produce a certain kind of society. Baby sitting, for instance, becomes a problem of major concern, as does education at the elementary level, and all sorts of social stratagems develop to meet problems such as these. But the resulting patterns of social behaviour can in no way be described as distinctively suburban in character. They are patterns of behaviour of all populations which move, of the population, for instance, of the Western Prairies in the years 1900-13, of the mining towns of Northern Ontario from 1920 to 1940.

This young population, without previous experience of home ownership and without any great accumulation of material resources, is also one suddenly faced with the task of building a community for itself without outside help. The drive to keep the price of the house down within the reach of the mass buyer determines the development of large-scale housing projects beyond that belt of country immediately surrounding the city where the price of land has been driven high by real-estate speculation. It determines further the nature of the development which takes place: the mass assembly of land and the construction and sale of all the homes in the subdivided area at the same time. Thus it is that there can be no easy extension of the social structure of old residential areas into the new, nor can there be, where all the residents arrive in the area at the same time, any relying upon the accomplishments, or the experience, of

---

In the township of Scarborough, for instance, in the area bounded by Victoria Park, Eglinton, Brimley, and Lawrence (census tracts 164 and 165), of a total population (twenty years of age and over) of 10,190 in 1956, 46 per cent fell in the age group twenty-five to thirty-four, and 76 per cent in the age group twenty-five to forty-four. In a typical residential area in the city of Toronto (census tract 81), out of a total adult population of 5,410, only 15.8 per cent was in the age group twenty-five to thirty-four and only 32.6 per cent in the age group twenty-five to forty-four. The age distribution of the population in the planned residential area is somewhere midway between that of the urban population and that of the mass-produced housing development. If the age distribution of the original residents (male) of Thorncrest Village and Regency Acres, a typical subdivision is compared, the difference is evident.

[14] Of the 379 families settling in Regency Acres, only sixty-two had previously owned homes. As would be expected, most of these were of the older age groups.

people already there.[15] The suburban is a society created almost literally overnight, and created out of only those limited materials the population has brought with it.

In such a society there is much, certainly, that a Riesman or a Whyte can deplore as there was much they could have deplored in the society of the Western Prairies in the early years of the century. This is not a society that can boast a strong interest in public affairs, in cultural activities, or in the development of gracious forms of living. Problems of concern to the population tend rather to have reference to the immediate struggle to establish a home and raise a family: problems of mounting property taxes, of roads breaking up with the spring thaw, of water-filled ditches along streets providing a hazard to children playing, of leaking basements and cracking plaster and the villainies of house builders, of over-crowded class-rooms, and the like. An intense dissatisfaction respecting matters which to an outsider may seem of little importance develops in a manner that may appear odd alongside an attitude of general complacency towards issues of great public significance.

But what must be stressed again is the youth of this population, undertaking for the first time to make a home and community for itself. It is treacherously easy for the well-established fifty-year-old to pass judgment upon the way the twenty-five-year-old starting out in life ought to live, but fortunately for the progress of the human race his judgment is not always able to prevail. The well-established fifty-year-old has a stake in the community. His status is closely identified with the organizational life of the community and the system of values upon which this organizational life depends. Thus the community in which there is a high degree of social participation comes to be thought of as the ideal community. Public spirit is judged a social good. Yet the vast majority of the young people moving into suburban residential areas clearly do not want to live in this kind of community at all. They couldn't care less for the kind of things offered by the planned residential area of the Don Mills or Thorncrest Village type. What they seek, rather, is an escape from

[15] There simply was no one in the subdivision of East Gwillimbury Heights before January 1958, while the location of the subdivision thirty miles north of Toronto and outside the town boundaries of Newmarket made for considerable social isolation in the first year or so after its establishment. The census figures show the same thing. The area in Scarborough township, for instance, enclosed by Victoria Park, Eglinton, Brimley, and Sheppard, had in 1951 a total of 1,081 families; in 1956 there were 12,615 families living in this area. There could not have been too many neighbours from whom to learn. On the other hand, in Thorncrest Village, it was ten years from the time the first house was built and occupied to the time that the last house was.

the kinds of demands and impositions which an old established community would place upon them.

There is, of course, on the part of such a population, no clear recognition of what it is escaping from. Rather, the population is one intent only upon the business at hand: the acquisition of a home in which to raise a family. But what this means is a very strong reluctance to get caught up in that kind of network of obligations which is a normal part of an old established society. To be left alone, that is as a family, is what is wanted more than anything else.

Thus those attributes which are identified with the suburban society in so much of the literature on suburbia are the very attributes which are the most conspicuously absent. In the planned residential area a great deal of "neighbouring" will be found. People here are organization-conscious and tend to observe carefully the conduct of their fellow-residents and to be ready to conform to what appear the accepted values of the group. Public spirit is much in evidence. But these are people whose very reason for moving into such residential areas is to discover a rich neighbourhood and community life. Where the investment in the home represents an investment as well in a particular way of life, community improvement as a means of protecting property values becomes a major consideration. Thus active participation in community life is an obligation readily accepted and, given the selective character of the population involved, one which imposes no insuperable burden.

In the mass-produced housing development, however, there will be found no such strong evidence of neighbouring, of participation in organizational activity, of conformity to the values of the group. This is a population excited by the fact of home ownership and taking very seriously its responsibilities as parents; but, contrary to the stereotype of suburbia, it is not a population anxious to become involved with neighbours, to join or attend meetings of organizations, to accept public office, or to engage in the costly undertaking of trying to "keep up" with other people in the community. Where the chief concern was the finding of a home priced within reach, there can be no consideration of community improvement as a means of protecting property values. Almost wholly lacking here is that upward mobility drive, made so much of by Whyte, which leads to the careful selection of the place to live, and its ready abandonment for another, in terms of one's status accomplishments and aspirations.

All which thus far has been said has reference, of course, to the suburban community which only just has come into being. In actual fact, no suburban community is so completely new that it displays nothing but the characteristics of the new community. From the very beginning, the old society intrudes, even if only a little, on the new; however isolated may be new mass-produced residential developments they do not grow up completely apart from older residential areas. And, with the passing of not more than a moment of time, the new suburban community becomes something of an old. Homes change hands, people move out and other people move in, and, though the difference between the newer and older home owners may not be great, there is a difference. However, even where a change of home ownership does not occur, the very passing of time produces a different people. Families begin to grow up, savings accumulate, the equity in the house becomes larger, and, with these and other changes in family circumstances, the stake in the community takes on a greater importance. There develops a pride in the home and in the neighbourhood. Concern shifts from problems narrowly centred in the house and family to problems of the larger social world in which the suburban resident finds himself becoming increasingly involved. The ratepayers' association withers away, its place taken by the community association or service club, neighbourhoods develop a new self-consciousness on the basis of social class or ethnic identity, participation in the social life of the larger community comes to consume an increasing proportion of the suburbanites time and energy. There is a vast difference between a suburban community ten years old and one newly born.

Indeed, it may be that in some of these ten-year-old communities characteristics of social life will be found not unlike those which in the literature have been identified with suburbia. But, if this is the case, the reason is not because these communities are suburban but because they are becoming urban. Probably no more highly urbanized area could have been found than the one selected by Seeley, Sim, and Loosley for study. The people who moved into Forest Hill Village were people who from the beginning could afford to maintain the complete gamut of urban services and, with it, the social supports of an urban way of life. Indeed, the very creation of the Village sprang from the desire to preserve urban values, or, more specifically, the values of an urban middle class, from the destructive forces of urban growth. The selective turn-over of population which later occurred, involving a very substantial change in the ethnic composition of the population, accentuated the urban character of the society. It was a highly urbanized people who replaced those who were the original home-owners. To some degree, there is this sort of selection, on the basis of identification with a particular set of urban values, of the population settling in all suburban areas, but this is only another way of saying that even in the most undifferentiated and unplanned of residential developments there is some carrying over of the urban social structure. What remains significant is the fact that this happens to a very much less extent in the mass-produced than in the planned housing development and that, in the former areas, it is only with the passing of time, that urban values enter prominently into the structuring of the society. At that point, but only then, the planned residential development built from the beginning about the values of the urban middle class becomes indistinguishable from the larger complex of middle-class society growing out of the suburbs.

The suburban becomes a part of the urban community but, in doing so, the whole of it by no means acquires the characteristics of an urban middle-class society. By the time the country-side surrounding the city is fully occupied, the city in truth has reproduced itself in the country. In the end, there is scarcely any element of the urban population which is not represented in the suburban. Here, certainly, besides the new middle-class societies it has brought into being, the city has given birth to new exclusive residential areas, working-class districts, colonies of ethnics, slums, criminal underworlds, and, indeed, even bohemias. To find here the "other-directed" or "organization" man would not, of course, be difficult as it would not be difficult to find all those other various types of men produced by a highly diversified kind of society that has now become urban. The society of "suburbia" has disappeared in becoming an urban society; but in reality such a society never existed except in the imagination of those persons who, in detecting certain social characteristics associated with the increasing importance of bureaucratic organization and mass communication in our society and discovering these characteristics in certain kinds of suburban areas, created the stereotype of suburbia.

To say this and nothing more about suburban development, however, is to skirt, it must be confessed, one of the main problems of such development. The suburban society may have none of the characteristics it has been made out to have. Yet its development, involving the growing up of vast residential areas outside the city, does pose problems of concern regarding the future welfare of urban society at large. The fact is that the country-side surrounding the city is being overrun by an urban population[16] and in a manner that appears highly wasteful from an economic and social point of view. It is not difficult to estimate some of the economic costs involved: the provision of transportation, sewerage, water, fire protection, education, shopping, police, and other such services in areas far removed from the main concentrations of population. The social costs, though less readily measured, are probably no less great. Society is the poorer as a result of the deprivations suffered by a suburban population: isolation, weakening of kinship ties, age imbalance, the consumption of its energy in the struggle to provide itself with housing and in getting to and from work, and an incapacity to support forms of intellectual or cultural expression. Indeed, it is scarcely possible to escape the feeling there is something almost fraudulent about the whole vast enterprise directed to the object of persuading people to move into the suburbs. There is a hiding of many of the real costs of such a movement: by municipal councils, in passing on to future tax-paying publics a part of the burden of providing services for the new suburban population; by the new residents themselves in postponing through first and even more second mortgages the charge upon their earnings of the house purchase; by a federal government in using financial aid to housing as a fiscal device; and by society at large which in the end must suffer the economic and social losses suburban development has entailed.

But the real question is not whether there are such losses but whether they are worth suffering, and this is a question upon which no final judgment can be passed. What is involved here is a matter of values about which there is no agreement. Indeed, the very use of such terms as "urban sprawl" is indicative of the kind of biases entering into much of the discussion of the problem of urban growth. Those who view with alarm the way our cities are being permitted to grow are too often people, like C. Wright Mills, for example, holding a strong belief in the virtues of planning. Such people don't like unplanned growth and as a consequence find no good in it.

What has to be demonstrated, from a sociological point of view, is whether under different conditions of development the economic and social losses resulting from urban growth would be lessened. In seeking an answer to this question, two facts must be kept clearly in mind. First, the vast majority of those families moving into the suburbs are families who can afford homes no more expensive than

[16] And by urban industry and commercial establishments, but discussion of this larger aspect of the problem lies beyond the scope of this paper.

those made available under present conditions of development. It becomes a question of whether it is possible to provide housing under more exacting conditions of planning—for instance, by preventing the leaping of subdivisions beyond that belt of undeveloped land surrounding the city, or by insisting upon a greater variety in housing designs or upon a more imaginative street lay-out,—and still keep it within the price reach of as many people. If it is not possible, the effect would be the elimination from the housing market of some of those people who are able to buy homes under prevailing conditions of development.

It can, of course, be argued that many of those people buying homes in the suburbs should be discouraged by price from doing so. Certainly, if aesthetic values had been the only consideration, one would have quickly settled for the Thorncrest Village model in the planning of the urban expansion of Toronto over the past ten years even if it had meant that only half as many people would have been housed in the suburbs as is now the case. But the social consequences of such a restriction upon housing development cannot be overlooked. In the fifteen years since World War II, to take an extreme case though one of considerable social significance, many thousands of impoverished families situated in the downtown overcrowded sections of Toronto have been able to secure homes for themselves by moving out into those cottage-type residential areas on the farthest periphery of the city. Such areas would quickly have been condemned by city planning and welfare departments had their jurisdiction reached so far. Their creation and continued existence have depended upon the tolerance of municipal councils made up of farmers or people with a farm outlook. It is easy to describe these cottage-type residential areas as blots on the landscape: they can boast no paved streets, well-cared-for lawns, public playgrounds for children, shopping centres, or homes that would pass even the most careless of building, fire, and health inspections. Indeed, the housing and public services in these areas would not come up to any generally accepted minimum standard of decency. Yet one cannot escape asking the question whether the people settled in these areas would have been as well off had they been unable to move out of the city. Here at least there is no smoke-laden air, sharing of housing, lack of open playing areas for children, or dependence upon services provided by an outside and alien world. By taking advantage of the opportunity to secure housing within their price range, people of impoverished circumstances have been able to build for themselves a home and a community in a way that was not possible in the city. This is not to say, of course, that such people could not have been provided with more adequate housing if society had been prepared to bear the cost. Nor is it to say that there were not other less wasteful ways of providing the housing that has been provided for these people, and even more for that very much larger number of people who have secured housing for themselves by locating in the new residential subdivisons growing up outside the city.

Considerations such as these, however, call attention to the second fact which must be kept in mind in seeking an answer to the question whether under different conditions of development the losses resulting from urban growth would be lessened. The population being provided with homes in the mass-produced housing areas outside the city is one possessed of certain very definite social preferences in terms of the way it wants to live. That is not to say that it has any precise ideas about housing designs, street lay-outs, or community plans. Nor is it to say that it is getting precisely what it wants in the housing market that has developed. But it would seem clear that the vast majority of people moving into the suburbs wants to live much, in fact, as it finds itself living. People who move to the suburbs want a home of their own; they want to be away from the confusion and the congestion of the big city; they want to be able to look out on open fields even knowing that these fields will soon disappear, and they want the anonymity which is provided by the big, unplanned, and socially non-centred residential development. Though they may not fully count the costs—the fatiguing and expensive daily trip to work, the onerous and mounting burden of mortgage payments and property taxes, the loneliness of subdivision life, the trials and tribulations of keeping a house in repair, particularly if it is improperly built, the lack of recreational facilities for children who have passed beyond school age, and the like—there is a readiness to accept the disadvantages of suburban life for the sake of the advantages. In another society, the urban society of Europe, for instance, people may want to live differently, and what thus is conceived of in our society as the good life might be considered intolerable in such a society as the European. We can learn much from the experience of city building of peoples in other lands but only if we recognize the differences as well as the similarities of the materials out of which the building is done.

In urging the importance of considerations such as these, there is no attempt to argue that planning is a bad thing or that the growth of our cities could not have been better planned. There can be no shutting one's eyes to the appalling waste of material and human resources which has resulted from the unrestricted growth of urban centres in past years. Indeed, a good deal of the energies of people living in cities is devoted to cleaning up the mess left them by people who have gone before, and this has always been so. But, while it is easy to calculate the costs of unrestricted development, it is not so easy to calculate the costs, on the other side, of planning and control. This is partly because the costs of unrestricted development are more economic while the costs of planning and control are more social. In part as well, however, it is because a hidden bias enters into the judgment of social costs. Even in the discussion of the nature of the process of urban growth there has been no complete escaping the stereotype of suburbia. It is hard not to believe that somehow or other life in the suburbs is not as desirable as life in the city. The ostensible grounds for the objection to the character of surburban development may be aesthetic, but underlying the aesthetic objection is one much more deeply rooted based on the feeling that people living in the suburbs are not living as they should.

Critics of the character of suburban development could not be expected, perhaps, to ask the question whether people in the suburbs are living as they want to live. But such critics could be expected to ask the question whether people in the suburbs are really living as they are made out to be. The stereotype of suburbia has done more than simply amuse the reader of the popular magazine or paperback book. It has entered into a good deal of the thinking about how our cities should be planned and what measures should be taken to assure a more satisfying urban way of life. Thus, to the extent that the stereotype has had no basis in reality, the effect has been to becloud the issues of urban growth and development.

The Social System of a Slum:
The Lower Ward, Toronto

W. E. MANN

SPEAKING in the Ontario Legislature, April 14, 1951, J. B. Salzberg, the member for St. Andrew's riding, Toronto, claimed "my riding is the most colourful, most dynamic, most cosmopolitan and most interesting of all ridings in the province." Continuing, he added, "there are slums in my riding. In the lower part there are areas that should have been cleared years ago."[1]

Here is how one resident of Salzberg's lower Ward describes the process of slum development:

When a city grows, "they" put the cream where the money is, and the garbage where they figure the garbage is . . . . What they should do is reverse the process! The way I see it, the slum is like shit, something you hide, put out of sight. I was born *down there;* I'm no bum, and a lot of guys born down there are not bums. Maybe I'm marked on account of being born down there, but that is all wrong, especially in today's world.

Another conception of life "down there" is furnished by a local hotel manager:

The people here go on from day to day because they have never been shown anything else. Their education has been very limited; they know nothing about the arts. They come to a point where they just exist and go right on at that level. They have had no real personal contact with anything better, so they just follow along from day to day. They don't seem to want to break away. They don't say, "Well, damn it, I've had enough of this, I'm going to get out of this and get something better." . . . This doesn't come into the minds of the majority.

They give and take, give and take and whatever they can grab, they'll take; they don't live on any principles. Their moral standard is low. A lot of them never clean up properly. They know they are dirty, so they just say, "well, to hell with it!" They live in a mood where improvement is something they just don't think about. In fact, they just don't think about anything too hard or too deep, but stay at a good safe level. What was alright last week will be alright this week.

[1] His riding included the colourful Spadina district, which was covered by *Maclean's* magazine in an article published July 6, 1957; the slum areas to which he refers (see Ontario Hansard, April 14, 1951) have not yet been cleared.

In the value system of Toronto's city fathers, and of the Metropolitan Toronto Executive, the lower Ward cuts little ice. Its population of about 8,000 persons counts for little politically; it has no influential citizens, and a small number turn out to vote. Although known to have many kinds of deviant activity, its crime is typically petty and not highly organized. While Jarvis Street in the east end and Dundas and Spadina, a mere quarter mile to the north, have been the subject of newspaper headlines demanding clean-ups, nobody has got very concerned about the bookmaking, prostitution, or juvenile delinquency in the lower Ward.

Before beginning a recent "survey" of the dope and vice rings allegedly focussed at Dundas and Spadina, Metropolitan Chairman F. G. Gardiner dropped into a hotel in our area. One observer reports:

He came down with four detectives . . . He has the idea . . . I guess I'll drop in and see what those birds are doing. So he comes in and sits down like a lord muckeddy muck; he's the whole cheese, he's going to look things over. I could stand it if he said to himself, "guess I've *got* to go down there, but I won't show how I feel" but he just sits up there, looking down on us. . . ."

The alleged attitude of Mr. Gardiner only reflects the status which Toronto puts on the lower Ward. Actually, this "corner" below Queen Street and from University to Shaw is, apart from its obvious commercial and industrial importance, a hidden "no man's land" to most respectable Torontonians. Swarming with business people, factory workers, cars, and trucks in the daytime, its busy thoroughfares like King, Richmond, Spadina, and Bathurst are deserted at night. Then the occasional visitor to the area may be easily frightened by the pervading bleakness and sense of desolation even on Queen Street which is much more illuminated than streets lower down.

But the lower Ward is not without significance to the city. Economically it includes the substantial Jewish garment industry, the huge Loblaws merchandising complex, the internationally known Massey-Harris-Ferguson plant, Tip Top Tailors, Molson's Brewery, and the main Toronto National Employment Service office, colloquially known as "the Slave Market." Its population, too, provides a large pool of unskilled labour which nearby plants, both large and small, find convenient. Its many rooming houses provide accommodation for hundreds of single men and its various hide-outs around truck depots and railway yards are used at night by many winos and transients who might otherwise spill over and cause embarrassment to more respectable areas. Also attractive to uptown people, some of whom work in the district, are certain night clubs which furnish "entertainment" and a certain night club flavour, not unaccompanied by "eager" female companions. Finally, the lower Ward is well known for its "Little Europe" of shops and stores, which draw to it weekly thousands of new Canadians intent on shopping for old country foods and similar items in their mother tongue.

TABLE I

ETHNIC GROUPS IN THE LOWER WARD (CENSUS TRACTS 49 and 63) 1951

Origin	Number	Percentage
British	4,086	40
French	617	6.0
Italian	370	3.7
German	125	1.2
Dutch	47	.5
Polish	1,653	16.4
Russian	165	1.6
Scandinavian	53	.5
Jewish	265	2.6
Ukrainian	1,457	14.4
Other European	889	8.8
Asiatic	235	2.3
Other, including Negro, Indian	203	2.0
TOTALS	10,165	100.0

Transitional zones are characterized by a great heterogeneity of population, and the lower Ward is no exception. Table I gives a breakdown of the ethnic groups for 1951; since then, more Hungarians, Japanese, and Portuguese have moved in, some Poles, Ukrainians, and Jews have left, but the gross heterogeneity has changed little. For instance, in one block of eleven houses in the centre of the area, there were in 1959 Macedonians, Poles, Ukrainians, Jews, Germans, Chinese, and Greeks as well as a coloured and an English family. In 1960 a careful estimate indicated that the Anglo-Saxons or "old Canadians" made up close to 40 per cent of the population, followed by Italians, Ukrainians, and Poles in that order, along with a fair sprinkling of Germans and central Europeans and a small number of Jews, Japanese, Portuguese, French-Canadians, Negroes, and Indians. Population heterogeneity is reflected in a considerable religious differentiation, although sects are noticeably absent. Table II gives the religious affiliations for 1951; although it is impossible to give a breakdown for 1960, little change appears to have occurred here since then.

TABLE II

RELIGIOUS DENOMINATIONS IN THE LOWER WARD (CENSUS TRACTS 49 and 63) 1951

Denomination	Number	Percentage
Baptist	316	3.0
Anglican	1,524	15.0
Greek Orthodox	627	6.1
Jewish	289	2.8*
Lutheran	289	2.8
Presbyterian	749	7.4
Roman Catholic	3,978	39.3
Ukrainian Greek Catholic	934	9.2
United Church	1,123	11.1
Others	336	3.3
TOTALS	10,165	100.0

*Certain Jews, listing themselves for religious purposes, changed their classification when asked for ethnic heritage.

Push and pull forces acting selectively have combined to change drastically the original ethnic and class character of the area. Although the area was almost entirely Anglo-Saxon and middle class before World War I, successive waves of Ukrainians, Poles, and Italians have "pushed" out the socially respectable and economically secure. Home-owning Anglo-Saxons, many still present in 1945, had by 1960 largely been replaced by home-owners of other ethnic groups or "old Canadian" renters. Many of the early European settlers have also sold out since the last war, and most recently Italians are moving up to replace Ukrainians and Poles as the largest new Canadian bloc.

The lower Ward's ecology is closely related to segregating forces operative in Toronto, as they are in every large city. Adjacent to the main railway tracks, heavily populated with truck depots, smoke-blackened industrial plants, and office buildings, and lying just west of the central business district, it is perhaps the least desirable residential section of Toronto. The air is heavily polluted, the side streets are littered or dirty, the roads are crammed all day with cars and lumbering trucks, most buildings, including churches and recreational facilities, are ugly or depressing, and the majority of the houses have deteriorated[2] or are sub-standard.

[2] This is less true of the district west of Bathurst Street.

The economically transitional character of this area is a consequence of its ecological situation. Socio-economic forces are pulling large offices and plants to uptown or suburban locations, numerous offices and small factories are hard to rent, and practically no new commercial buildings have been built in fifteen years. Houses are being torn down at the rate of ten to twenty a year, principally to meet parking demands, and the population is steadily declining. The whole district, too, is zoned commercial-industrial, which means that no new housing whatsoever may be built—a Planning Department policy that dooms the lower Ward to old, worn-out housing and eventual extinction as a residential area. Meantime, as some established firms move out, the district slowly fills up with those types of business concerns to which convenience and accessibility to the downtown streets are crucially important.

Situational factors are decisive in selecting the population that is drawn to, and remains in, the lower Ward. The area's low social status, bleak physical appearance, confused moral climate, and residential and social instability tend to attract persons and families sharing one or more of the following characteristics: weak intelligence, poor physical health, low social or economic status, disorganized or unstable personalities, or strong feelings of social protest. Among these one finds the physically or mentally handicapped,[3] the psychologically ill,[4] the very poor, compulsory drinkers and alcoholics, deserted wives, common-law households, and other moral non-conformists, bootleggers, thieves, and families of mixed racial heritage.

Specific institutions both legitimate and illegitimate also operate selectively to draw in certain types of residents. Flop houses and cheap rooming-houses, most numerous just above Queen Street, are augmented by a dozen hotels with rooms to rent, besides hundreds of households that take in roomers or boarders to supplement the family income.[5] These facilities explain why the 1956 census recorded 1553 unmarried males and a total of 4,962 men as compared to 3,610 women in the area. Considerable rental housing, much of it owned by a few absentee landowners or handled by trust companies and available to families regardless of size for comparatively moderate

[3] In one school of 300 pupils, two of the seven classes are opportunity classes, which means the children in them are below 90 I.Q.
[4] This area has just about the highest mental illness rate for the Metropolitan area. See Diane Jaffey, "Ecology and Mental Disease in Toronto," MSW thesis, University of Toronto, School of Social Work, 1956.
[5] According to the 1956 census, 750 out of 1493 households take in lodgers.

rentals, tends also to concentrate in the lower Ward a significant number of large families, owing in part to the scarcity of such accommodation in most other parts of Toronto. According to the 1956 census, there were 119 families with five children or more.

Another important characteristic is a high degree of anonymity. On certain streets as many as three families, together with several single individuals, will live in one three-storey house and members of one family may not know the names of members of another. A similar anonymity is characteristic of certain streets where the houses are not close together, but separated by parking lots or commercial buildings. This situation allows individuals and even families to hide out or become "lost" to relatives, creditors, or enemies, and thus commends the area to certain types of people.

Economically and socially the lower Ward is an area of minimal competition; for many residents it is a place of final retreat from socio-economic or personality failures. As one informant put it:

They're here because they can't make a go of it elsewhere, something like the Eskimos or other tribes living under very hard conditions. It's been found that rather than fight it out with people in other areas, it is easier to sort of retire to an inhospitable area, . . . you've got the ground there to yourself. . . . I think it's a feeling of not quite being able to get along and hold one's own among other people.

In the lower Ward such people are relatively safe, that is, un-threatened. By the same token, those who attain a little higher degree of economic, moral, or organizational stability become uncomfortable and move to a more congenial district. (A few people of the European ethnic groups in their late fifties or sixties are exceptions to this, hanging onto their homes and fearful of new changes.) These are usually replaced by families from east-end slums or from slum or low status districts of towns in Ontario, the Maritimes, or occasionally the West.

Most of the mobility within the lower Ward is within the area itself, a fact borne out by examination of moving patterns of school children. However, a sizeable percentage move to east-end slums, and something like 15 per cent of the movers in a given year shift to a higher status district. The rate of mobility is also characteristically high. In one school, the children turn over almost 100 per cent in a ten-month school year. Of this turnover, 75 per cent is attributable to only 25 per cent of the families, the "hard core" types who through sheer economic pressure may move three or even four times in a year. This group, especially, merely shifts residence a few blocks away within the neighbourhood.

Since the depression, ecological forces have tended to concentrate two types of residents in this area: impecunious or low status immigrants, and low status "old Canadians." In this paper attention will be focussed on the latter. Although members of this group may have some limited friendship ties with new Canadians, usually as neighbours or drinking friends at the neighbourhood pub, generally speaking "old Canadians" refuse to mix with immigrants of other ethnic groups. Their expression is "we don't bother with them." On many streets where new Canadians predominate, this practice of "minding one's own business" results in a considerable degree of social isolation for "old Canadians." When the immigrants begin to "take over" a particular street, the residual "old Canadians" express their hostility at being pushed out in various ways, such as stigmatizing the immigrants as "D.P.'s" or "dirty foreigners," or refusing to patronize new Canadians' stores along the side street or on Queen. Occasionally, hostility erupts in violence. On one street a ferocious physical conflict occurred in 1959, the police arriving after several hours of fighting just in time to prevent the use of knives and guns.

Voluntarily segregated from European immigrants, the "old Canadians" are also cut off socially from the larger Anglo-Saxon community of Toronto. Just living in the lower Ward means they are stigmatized as slum dwellers. Thus one rather exceptional housewife of the district who boards Children's Aid foster children and meets frequently with other such women, from "up there," said she receives many curious questions, such as, "How could you *ever* live in a district like that?" A successful storekeeper from Queen Street reflected the attitude of the average Torontonian towards the "old Canadians" when he called them in an interview, "white trash," and then hastily changed the expression to "cheap English." It is widely believed that all the "old Canadians" here must be shiftless, ignorant, dirty, unmannered, and given to foul language, sexual licence, and huge families.

Social distance between the slum and the non-slum in Toronto is reflected in the expressions, "up there" and "down here." The usage "down here" reflects the residents' concept of their lowered status. Hostility to the population "up there" is indicated by the following statement of one resident,

Up there a lot of people are trying for something–I don't know what. At least 'down here' there's a sort of truth and basic reality. . . . There's no use putting on the old BS down here, because if you haven't got it, you ain't got it, and that's all there is to it.

In sum, the "old Canadians" are segregated both from the surrounding residents of another ethnic culture, and from the respectable working or middle class community of greater Toronto. They are an outcast group.

Within the total body, however, two distinct subgroups of "old Canadians" may usefully be distinguished. The first and much smaller one is made up of Anglo-Saxons who, while identifying with the area, commonly through long residence, still maintain some connections with the larger Toronto community, usually through institutional allegiances. They tend to accept standards of responsibility, morality, or entertainment belonging to "up there"; they also usually possess as reference groups organizations or institutions such as a church whose roots and orientation are "up there." In most cases these individuals are largely marginal to the slum society, sharing essentially upper working-class attitudes and values and living in considerable isolation from indigenous slum institutions and codes. While frequently exhibiting what might be considered leadership traits from a non-slum standpoint—for example, intelligence, organizing ability, or broad social insights—their marginal situation undermines any opportunity of their performing leadership functions with the main "old Canadian" group.

The predominant group of "old Canadians" may be considered as of the lower lower class, using Warner's classification,[6] provided it is clear that this does not signify any identifiable class consciousness as such. They are lower in the sense that they are in the lowest social rank and usually at "the point of no return." As one informant indicated, "The people here feel defeated...beat! Here they are and they don't think they can get out—they've grown up in *this kind of an area* and it's all they know." Educationally they may have attained grade eight, occupationally they are stuck in non-skilled trades or find themselves frequently unemployed, and in income, although a few make $80 a week, the majority earn less than $3,000 a year. In health, in social intelligence, and in achievement they also tend to fall into the very lowest bracket. Perhaps a more descriptive term than lower lower class is socially residual, since it avoids misleading class overtones and suggests a highly generalized lower social status.

[6] W. L. Warner, M. Meeker, and K. Eells, *Social Class in America* (Chicago, 1949).

Just above Queen Street, the boundary of this area, the picture is significantly different. A local school principal with experience both north and south of Queen Street described this difference as follows:

Above Queen the population is more heterogeneous than here, more new Canadian and Negro. . . . Their new Canadians in the main tend to be more ambitious; they have a greater desire to learn and get ahead. Their area too is more residential. . . . A considerable number who transfer from the school there, transfer to "better" districts. That's the chief reason for their student turnover, whereas here the reasons for turnover are different. Also we have two opportunity classes with less than 300 children; they have only one for 1,200 children.

In brief, the area below Queen seems to "trap" or "shelter" residual "old Canadians" who not only are barred from upward movement by deficiencies of various types, but who are typically fearful of venturing out of their neighbourhood. One informant indicated, "The majority of the youngsters and adults down here tend to be rather a beaten down group."

Fundamental to their adjustment process and the resulting social system is the precarious economic situation of the "old Canadian" group. Lacking saleable skills or educational qualifications, this group enters the employment market heavily handicapped. The young boys, fresh out of grade eight or nine, are forced to take any job, such as that of delivery boy, messenger, or unskilled labourer in a factory. To be "big enough" to earn money is very important to the teen-ager; the amount at the beginning is less significant. The young men typically change jobs frequently, quitting abruptly over hurt feelings, or being fired by "fed-up" bosses. In the process of job hunting, vague notions of qualifying for semi-skilled or apprentice-ship-requiring jobs are gradually defeated and a significant percentage end up as truck drivers.[7]

Many factors urge this choice on the younger men. In the first place, since the area is dotted with truck depots, this work is convenient, an important factor in the lower Ward; also, word of openings travels quickly along the grapevine, for instance, in the pubs. Although among the bigger companies the trend is towards careful screening of applicants and an emphasis upon stable, young married men, much hiring is still casual or somewhat haphazard. Secondly, for various reasons this occupation has more prestige than factory employment: it is more masculine, is outside rather than inside, gives

[7] An analysis of the 1958 provincial voters' list for this area indicated that about 15 per cent of the men, the largest proportion in any given occupation, were drivers.

the individual more freedom and sense of independence, involves more variety and excitement. Thirdly, it has advantages over comparable jobs in providing opportunities, for instance, for regular short stop-offs, commonly made at grills or beer parlours, for contacts with promiscuous females and often for extra earnings through overtime.[8] Long-haul trucking in particular, which involves out-of-town driving, boasts all of the above "rewards" in addition to a general high status in the truckers' world.

Thus truck driving tends to select men who claim they "can't stand indoor work," who want a sense of independence on the job, are mechanically inclined, and also value a sense of belonging. As an occupational group, truckers share a common work experience and a system of values and work codes that serves along with their union and its drinking club—in the east-end slums of Toronto—to integrate them more than many lower status work groups. One pub manager spoke of the drivers who regularly gather in his pub: "They come in and they laugh it up. They talk to one another over the tables, maybe three or four tables away; there seems a much closer association [than among other groups]. They seem to have more things to talk about." Those issued with distinctive uniforms by their companies, Loblaw drivers for instance, especially give signs of a strong sense of status and group unity.

Certain aspects of truck driving are functional to the value system of the young Anglo-Saxons in the lower Ward, for example, the convenient location of the work itself. This fits in with the common emphasis placed on avoiding great effort, and also facilitates identification with the neighbourhood and its small insulated social world. Relative freedom on the job and lack of careful supervision also permit a casualness of attitude that accords well with the social temper of the lower Ward and its norm of impulse gratification. The appeal of the excitement and danger involved in daring driving is not to be underrated, and clearly answers the conditioned need for excitement. In certain types of trucking, accidents are quite frequent. One long-haul driver told the writer: "Four of my chums have been killed in the last year. The last one was crushed while loading at the back of a truck." It is easy to see how truck driving would appeal to the youth of the lower Ward, conditioned to a life of accidents, mobility, danger, and thrills in boyhood. In fact, the cultural complex surrounding the truck driver's work life, with its considerable group identification and pub-centred recreation, its expression of impulse,

[8] As piggy-back hauling becomes more popular, overtime is being cut down.

and its casual acceptance of illegal violence,[9] not excluding wildcat strikes, is fundamentally identical with much of the social climate of life in the lower Ward.

In its impact upon the family and other social institutions this occupation is also significant. Whereas its long and often erratic work hours undercut opportunities to play supportive roles in the family, its focus on the pub and drinking codes fosters identification with all-male groups and with the local pub as a second home. A male culture is accented separate from the female-housekeeper-mother culture. The truckers' way of life and erratic hours of work also militate strongly against participation in formal meetings and associations and favour the casual, primary group kinds of social participation characteristic of slum society.

Up to 50 per cent of employed "old Canadians" not engaged in trucking have jobs that involve considerable overnight or shift work which likewise disrupts family life and formal social participation. Night watchmen, porters, janitors, foundrymen, and those in similar low status jobs have to accept their turn on undesirable shifts. One housewife expressed a common female reaction, "When he's on the night shift, he's too beat to bother with the children; I have to do everything." This puts the responsibility on the wife-mother to hold the family together. A similar situation tends to prevail where, as is frequent in the lower Ward, the father is disabled or unemployed, or has deserted the wife. In 1959 some seventy families and ninety single individuals were receiving welfare, twenty to thirty families were on Mother's Allowance, forty to fifty individuals or heads of families were on old age or disabled pensions, and at least fifty individuals, mainly heads of families, were receiving unemployment insurance.[10] Altogether between 125 and 150 families were dependent upon governmental assistance. Here again family and associational relationships were probably severely disturbed.[11]

The economically marginal situation of the "old Canadians" shapes the social system at various levels. It affects family stability through the widespread practice of subletting: most of the households of three to six children are squeezed into half of a six-room house, with the upstairs rented to another family or to single individ-

[9] When violence is in the air, pitching bricks through windshields is not uncommon among some truck drivers.
[10] It was impossible to get precise data from the appropriate authorities on this item. An analysis of the voters' list for the 1958 provincial election indicated that from 5 to 10 per cent of the men in this area claimed unemployment at that time.
[11] E. W. Bakke, *The Unemployed Worker* (New Haven, 1940).

uals. It stimulates borrowing and lending of food and household utensils between neighbours and the use of the neighbourhood grocery store where credit is provided. While these latter practices help to focus socio-economic activity upon the small neighbourhood, they often lead to strained relationships rather than good neighbourhood integration. Low and uncertain incomes also encourage buying things on time in this area. A large percentage of families are harassed by debts which often run from $500 to $1,000 per family. Codes governing borrowing and lending between housewives have their counterpart in the neighbourhood pub where the regulars, particularly work partners, make loans to one another. Here the code of repayment, usually on payday, is rigidly observed. Interestingly enough, credit unions which two churches organized in the 1950's failed to win substantial interest among the "old Canadians."[12]

It is customary for "old Canadians" to expect loans and even gifts of cash from local churches. Transients and families on welfare resort to clergy most frequently, but other "old Canadians" are not adverse to buttonholing the clergymen for money or gifts of food and clothing. The churches of the area—Presbyterian, Salvation Army, Anglican, United, and Roman Catholic—are all heavily committed to such assistance. In fact, along with extensive children's recreational activities economic assistance bulks largest in their weekly programme.[13] One Presbyterian church besides giving meal tickets away to the value of $30 a month—to any Scotsman who is hard up—also hands out over $200 a year in cash and grocery orders in addition to a large amount of clothing and several hundred Christmas baskets. One Anglican church recorded over $2,000 in cash donations in 1957 in addition to large quantities of clothing. A Roman Catholic church averaged about ten requests a day from transients in 1958 and often gave $1.50 to each. In addition, its St. Vincent de Paul Society gives considerable economic assistance to needy families and operates a second-hand clothing store on Queen Street where prices are characteristically low. The Salvation Army runs a large hostel for men in the area as well as a large clothing and furniture depot at bargain store prices. It is estimated that up to 1958 the churches altogether gave annually upwards of $5,000 in cash or meal tickets and another $5,000 in food and clothing. (Christmas

---

[12] The United Church Credit Union was popular, however, with congregations of other ethnic groups and helped them in social ascent. Credit unions are too formalized, too dependent upon secondary associational experience, too integrated with the world of "up there" to gain strong support from "old Canadians."
[13] The local ethnic churches characteristically are not recipients of many such requests.

funds and baskets also would easily run to another $10,000.) Prot-
estant church rummage sales, their most popular social function
and money raising effort, must also be classified as an indirect form
of assistance to those on the margin of subsistence.

Two missions almost entirely devoted to welfare work also give
annually thousands of dollars of assistance. The Evangel Hall, a
Presbyterian mission, feeds over 100 men including transients, old-
age pensioners, and alcoholics every evening with free sandwiches,
buns, and coffee, and gives away considerable clothing and food to
families. The Scott Mission[14] with a permanent staff of fifteen, located
on Spadina half a mile north of Queen Street, feeds 200 men twice a
day and averages twenty grocery and fifteen clothing donations daily,
about one-quarter to one-third of which go to lower Ward residents.

The attitude of many "old Canadians" towards church hand-outs
is "Grab all you can." This code is illustrated by the way in which
Sunday School Christmas parties and the Christmas basket operation consistently involve cheating on a wholesale basis. The operation of this norm tends to victimize the churches which liberally give
away money, food, or clothing and confirms their marginal position
in the local social system. The fact that residents have no conception
of the actual source of hand-outs or the limitations on their volume
strengthens the notion that clergy and churches are fair game.

One resident expressed a typical attitude towards the church when
he said, "If I went inside your church the walls would fall down."
Another expressed a fairly common view when he said, "A lot of the
guys look on the church as something for the birds; some have even
got a great hatred for it." Some "old Canadians" are too proud or
hostile to ask churches for any help, but the majority will use them
for economic assistance or recreation for children while refusing to
support Sunday services or mid-week organizations. Interviews of a
sample of residents and analysis of church attendance records indicate that less than 10 per cent of the "old Canadians" and less than
5 per cent of their menfolk attend church regularly. Thus, the local
United Church with two large, well-equipped buildings, a staff of
four, and a $24,000 budget counted less than ten men from the area
as regular church supporters. Also lay leadership, even in Roman
Catholic organizations, tends to be given by ex-residents of the area
who come down on Sundays from "up there."[15] On the other hand

---

[14] See an article in *Maclean's* magazine, "Anybody Eats Here Free" (Sept. 17, 1955)
[15] Those who go are usually the more ambitious ones who will soon leave the area,
or the quieter, more organized, and more respectable types.

except for the Italians, the local new Canadians have a fair church attendance record.

The economic aid rendered by social agencies and the local public schools likewise fails to gain these institutions full acceptance from the local population. In spite of systematic donations of shoes and clothing for needy children[16] and generous Christmas party gifts, parents accorded local schools little co-operation. In fact, by both children and parents the school is generally regarded as the spokesman for an alien ideology and culture. This is reflected in such things as the comparatively high rate of absenteeism,[17] the infrequency of parental calls at the school, and the impossibility of organizing Home and School associations.

Social agencies and their workers in spite of frequent handouts are also the objects of distrust or exploitation. By unspoken agreement, the city welfare department, Mother's Allowance, and other such welfare agencies are generally exploited to the limit. Behind this practice lies the belief that these institutions are fair game since they represent an alien or hostile social system. Frequency of cheating leads some welfare workers to snoop—occasionally dropping in at unreasonable hours—in the hope of securing decisive evidence. Such manoeuvres, or the enforcement of what appear as unreasonable regulations, increase the resentment of welfare recipients. The following statement by Mrs. B., the landlady of a welfare recipient Mrs. L., who rented upstairs rooms from her and who at the time of the interview was sitting in the room, records this reaction:

We resent the way the welfare workers snoop around and also the regulations that you can't even work part time and still get relief. Mrs. L's worker is against her helping me and is always asking what I pay her. Early one morning the worker came to the house without even knocking; she simply opened the door and said, "Anybody home?" and began walking upstairs to Mrs. L's rooms. My husband got up from bed in a hurry, very mad, and said, "You know it's not right to come in without knocking." The worker went upstairs anyway and found Mrs. L. in the bed in my son's room. He's married you know, but his wife left him some years ago for a coloured man. She said to Mrs. L., "What's the idea, why aren't you in the room with your children?" Mrs. L. said the children had measles and that my son had given her permission to sleep in his room to avoid catching the germs as he was out of town for awhile.

Support for social agencies or the schools is similarly limited even in the Roman Catholic separate school with 980 pupils. To quote

[16] These were usually secured from uptown schools.
[17] The attendance in one school was 91 per cent as compared to a city-wide average of 96 per cent.

one assistant priest, "A parent-teacher organization is out of the question. The parents wouldn't show up. They are not interested in their kids' education."[18] This judgment, of course, stems from an ethnocentric middle-class outlook, in which education is *ipso facto* given a high value; in the lower Ward value system, schooling is not ranked high and therefore many parents take little interest in their children's educational advance. Similarly, public school pupils tend to resent schools, evade homework consistently, and fail frequently; many are still in grade eight at age fifteen years. One informant, not yet thirty, recalling his school days, said, "Often when I go by Niagara School I'd like to put a bomb under it. It was like a sadistic hole."

Hostility towards educational and other institutions such as churches and social agencies is not untypical of slum areas. Thus Myers and Roberts, writing in *Family and Class Dynamics in Mental Illness* of lower class (category V) patients, note that "most display a deep-seated distrust of institutions and persons of authority."[19] Other American studies of slum residents and neighbourhoods support this conclusion and confirm the existence of a value system at cross purposes with that of the dominant middle-class community.

In general, the operation and structure of schools, churches, and social agencies[20] in the lower Ward insistently identify them with "up there." They represent to the "old Canadians" the clean, law-abiding, educated, organized, and successful society of the "haves" from which they are excluded. In practice, they operate as institutions of social control, aiming at the conformity of residents with the goals and codes of the larger community. The functionaries charged with operating these institutions together constitute a loosely interwoven group fundamentally alien to the value and social systems of the residents of the lower Ward. The police—considered by local teenagers and many adults as their natural enemies—are regarded by most such officials as colleagues on the job. Also, such functionaries inevitably consult back and forth about mutual interests and problems and tend to defend one other against criticisms of local residents. Practically all of the teachers, doctors, clergymen, and social workers live outside the lower Ward, travel "down"

[18] This does not apply to certain immigrant groups.
[19] Jerome K. Myers and Bertram H. Roberts, *Family and Class Dynamics in Mental Illness* (New York, 1959), p. 185.
[20] There is no settlement house in the lower Ward and the two which are a mere two or three blocks north of Queen Street are considered well outside the neighbourhood and draw very few young people on a regular basis.

to it each day, accept the codes and pecuniary advancement goals of the larger community, and possess a self-image of themselves as professional or semi-professional workers, an occupational "cut" far above that of lower Ward residents. They also share a somewhat common work situation, in which feelings of discouragement resulting from an incapacity to understand local norms and behaviour patterns and their social distance from residents are often mingled with feelings of inadequate social or personal recognition, and of hostility towards certain goals or doctrines of headquarters. Moreover, these functionaries tend to act consistently as members of bureaucratic organizations, whose universalistic norms, impersonal forms of control, rules of procedure, and allegiance to secondary types of associations cut across the values and ways of life of the local social system and culture. In fact, the very emphasis put by these powerful institutions upon formal, secondary, and largely impersonal relationships may indeed accentuate the primary group, informal particularistic bases of the "old Canadian" lower Ward social system.

In a sense, these institutions and functionaries may be likened to an "occupying force" in a conquered territory, operating under orders, both explicit and implicit, from army headquarters in the home country. Here, specific directives are, of course, issued from separate bureaucratic centres (church, police, and social agency headquarters) not commonly under one explicit directorate, but consultations on policy and problems are not uncommon. Here, also, functionaries have their base in buildings neither built nor financially maintained by lower Ward residents, are paid salaries by outside, largely alien bureaucratic institutions,[21] and generally regard their work in the lower Ward as both different from and much more demanding than that in most other areas of Toronto. In addition, they usually identify themselves with uptown and regard their stint or activity in the area variously as "difficult," "trying," "disciplinary," or as a necessary step in the process of professional advancement. Occasionally, a few may see it as "fascinating" or adventurous.

In handling the welfare problems that often bring together teachers, clergymen, social workers, policemen and even civic officials, these functionaries understand and accept the rules and norms of bureaucratic investigation and decision. This rationalized structure, readily accepted if occasionally criticized by the functionary, constitutes a completely dark and forbidding world to old and new

[21] Except for the Roman Catholics, church collections pay only a small fraction of clergymen's salaries.

Canadian residents alike. When the residents criticize this world, the functionary, even if constrained to sympathize, feels he must try to interpret it constructively, and in so doing implies his identification with it. Such interpretations frequently deepen the gulf between functionary and slum resident, rather than clarifying it.

The task of an occupying force is seldom free from strain, and in the process of meeting the situation adjustments are usually made with respect to orders and directives from headquarters and their implementation. In coming to terms with the lower Ward's culture, institutional workers typically modify the goals and standards they are supposed to support and also attempt to get "headquarters" to adopt more realistic policies. Occasionally, this accommodation involves a process of partial acceptance of certain codes and goals well-entrenched in the indigenous social system. This adjustment and partial identification in turn makes functionaries critical of certain rigidities within their bureaucratic apparatus and may lead to serious strains and stresses, hidden or overt. The social distance of headquarters personnel from the actual situation and people of the lower Ward, whether it be civic departmental heads, church headquarters officials, or school administrators, is at the root of those inappropriate goals and standards which sustain tension between functionaries in the "occupying force" and their superiors in the bureaucracy.

Such tensions are most obvious among the clergy, faced with great discouragements in securing support and making converts. While Roman Catholic priests are most critical of headquarters' policy with regard to the ethnic Catholic churches of the area—which refuse to die gracefully at the second generation stage—non-Roman Catholic clergy tend to attack the central authorities because of niggardly financial grants, inadequacies of staff, or indifference to the need for new policies. One young minister expressed a common complaint:

If you could only get through to "them." Any request (for a change) has to go through various levels of authority. We don't have direct contact with the real persons with the power. A minister I know said he left the ministry—for social work—because he couldn't get enough support. . . . A policy of thrift still dominates the thinking of our leaders, and they are too little daring.

Similar tensions, although usually less acute, afflict local workers in schools, the welfare department, the city-run recreational centre, and the police force. For instance, whereas the district Mother's Allowance supervisor may be vigorously orientated to keeping down welfare payments and may have his own tricks to catch and disqualify unwary applicants, field workers sympathize with many welfare recipients and often wink at the heavy drinkers who should be reported and penalized. Complaints made to the writer by local recreational workers and police officials indicate a similar lack of agreement with headquarters policy.

Thus the adjustment of the alien institutions to social realities in the lower Ward is seriously handicapped by the bureaucratic process and the social distance of high-level functionaries, trapped and sheltered in a highly rational middle-class bureaucratic world, distant from the peculiar needs of the "occupied" territory.

In 1959, two institutions with uptown affiliations, by cutting themselves off to a great degree from "headquarters," succeeded in meeting significant local needs and in so doing throw light upon the indigenous social system. One was a free Medical Clinic run at St. John's Anglican Church in the south central part of the area, and operated in loose affiliation with both that church and the nearby Western Hospital. Begun in 1923, the Clinic gave attention for four half-days per week to a variety of simple medical needs including pre-natal care, infants' diseases, immunization, eye glasses for children and adults, and minor illnesses and accidents. It served 80 to 100 patients a week and accepted anyone. Faced with a threat of closure from hospital authorities in 1958, study revealed that its local appeal lay in being a neighbourhood institution, convenient, simple, unpolished, and informal in appearance, and in providing more personalized and efficient attention, with a minimum of red tape and a much smaller fee than the public clinic at the nearby[22] Western Hospital. The fact that both the church and the Clinic had severed practically all ties with the diocese years before kept the Clinic free from denominational and bureaucratic controls; the presence on its reception staff of persons born and raised in the area increased its acceptability and identification with residents of the lower Ward.

The Stanley Park (Civic) Recreation Centre, in the southwest corner of the district, was until 1959 the focus for a tremendous amount of recreation for youngsters up to sixteen living west of Bathurst Street. When the Massey-Harris-Ferguson Company decided in 1960 to buy the property for additional parking space, local residents raised a storm of protest. Nothing in the previous fifteen years so mobilized local opinion as this threat to the residents of the loss of "their" recreational centre. The city's argument that a new,

---

[22] The hospital is about a third of a mile north of Queen Street, on Bathurst Street.

polished, one million dollar social centre was nearing completion on Trinity Park grounds, just north of Queen Street, did not satisfy them. Stanley Park was a *neighbourhood centre* housed in an appropriately ugly, old red-brick building, formerly a bank, with a programme including boxing, tumbling, hockey, baseball, swimming, pingpong, and basketball, which kept hundreds of children active after school hours. It had a staff, headed by an Irishman raised in a working-class area in the east end of Toronto, which identified with the people, drank beer with the men in the local pubs, and *protected their secrets* (for instance, the location of bootleg dealers and gatherings of winos). Many old boys from Stanley Park had sent their sons back to play hockey or baseball on the Stanley Park teams—and their victories reflected glory on the district. The new institution on Queen was just out of the neighbourhood, too polished and bright to be "their" centre; it would inevitably belong, for some time at least, to the alien world of "up there." So the struggle for the old Stanley Park Centre was a fight for personal, neighbourhood, particularistic values against the impersonal, alien bureaucratic world of "up there." However, protests in the press were all in vain; the centre is now demolished.

The social system of the "old Canadians" of the lower Ward may be regarded at this point as an ambivalent structure hostile to but dependent upon the middle-class culture predominant in Toronto. The encircling community possesses the great preponderance of power and impresses its main values, goals, and codes upon all members. Certain ecological factors, however, tend to weaken the impact of such values, goals, and codes upon the lower Ward. Here there is a cultural derogation of the educational system, a widespread indifference to reading, including the daily newspaper[23] and popular magazines—except perhaps for love and murder stories—and an intense concentration of interest and activity upon the local neighbourhood. The significant social world of lower Ward residents is an area of perhaps four to five blocks square; beyond this is largely foreign territory. Indifference to secondary associations, which encourage mobility and diffusion of interests, and insulation within certain local institutions like the pub further strengthen the isolation of these residents from middle-class influences.

Nonetheless, to an important degree, old Canadian residents of the lower Ward are still exposed to the principal goals of the larger

[23] Interviews with a random sample of residents indicated that very few read popular magazines, and less than 50 per cent take a daily newspaper.

community, while being denied access to means of pecuniary and social ascent. This dissociation between goals and available means leads generally to the following types of reaction: (1) Feelings of frustration producing a general proclivity towards verbal or physical violence, evidenced most frequently in beer parlour fights, and towards escape patterns, notably heavy drinking and sexual promiscuity; (2) a withdrawal from social and political responsibilities, evidenced by profound indifference to current events, non-reading of newspapers, and excessive electoral apathy, along with a lack of interest in voluntary associations aimed at community improvement; (3) an orientation towards minimal economic security rather than the culturally prescribed goal of socio-economic ascent (in seeking mere subsistence, many middle-class codes may be partially jettisoned, for example, legal codes against bookmaking or bootlegging, cheating of welfare workers, or sharing limited housing accommodation with strangers); (4) an ideology of living for the moment, elevating whim and impulse above middle-class norms of budgeting, thrift, and care for the future; and (5) a concentration of social participation upon small informal groups, such as the family, the gang, the work or the pub group, which are functional to adequate social adjustment within the lower Ward situation.

One focal point of the local social system, the family and "extended" kin group, emerges as a significant institution. Among lower Ward "old Canadians" the family is characteristically weak in authority, more matriarchal than patriarchal, loosely integrated, and the scene of a great deal of open conflict. Romance is not intensive before marriage and soon disappears altogether, giving place to a sexual dichotomy in which men and women build up and live in separate, almost water-tight cultures. Family codes have little in common with those of middle-class families. Children learn to swear profusely at four or five years of age, pick up the "facts of life" before ten, usually have their first sexual experience by twelve or thirteen, may leave home temporarily or permanently at sixteen, and consider marriage seriously at sixteen for girls and eighteen for boys. Illegitimate children are not uncommon—although low in numbers in view of early sexual activity—and are often raised in the grandparental household. Parents show little interest in or control over their children's play and friendship behaviour and are usually content to let them wander the streets or where possible attend church or school clubs. Up to one-third of the couples in certain streets live in common-law relationships. Broken homes are fairly common as is supervision by Children's Aid societies.[24] After a few years of marriage, periodic sexual prosmiscuity, often with neighbours, beer parlour acquaintances, or pick-ups, becomes a frequent pattern and meets few informal punitive sanctions.

Such a loose family system is largely an accommodation to socio-economic imperatives. Crowded living quarters leave no room for children to bring in friends, with the result that the street or the recreational club becomes the real home. Precociously early sex experiences and early marriage quickly rub off the romantic element in sex relationships and emphasize physical and social compatibility. The many frustrations of low status existence put a premium on liquor and sex as releases. Dissociation from middle-class success goals leaves families with no strong orientation towards intensive child care or training or the repression of aggressive impulses. The financial impossibility of securing a divorce fosters common-law alliances.

Closely associated with the nuclear family, and particularly with the mother, are usually several kin[25] who live in or close to the lower Ward. Weekly or more frequent visits of the mother-in-law or other such members of this "extended" kin group are common, and one or more of such relations sometimes live with the family. Participation in this larger kin group and support from it in times of emergency are an important characteristic of the lower Ward social system. Interviews with a representative sample of residents indicated that this pattern is true for some 70 per cent of the families; in the majority of these one or more relatives lived within a mile or two of the nuclear family. In such interviews, the following was a typical answer to the question, "Do you have close relatives living close by?" "Yes, we have relatives nearby; one in the east end, and one near the Western Hospital. One drops in three times a week. Several others who live further away come once or twice a month." The greater majority of such kin alignments are from the mother's family; apparently a major function of such relationships is to support her in the absence of close integration with the husband, whose strongest bonds are often with males at his place of work or at the local pub.

What the extended kin group does in support of the family and specifically the mother, the teen-age gang does for the adolescent

[24] In 1959, 50 Roman Catholic and 29 Protestant families were under Children's Aid supervision.
[25] See Morris Axelrod, "Urban Structure and Social Participation," *American Sociological Review*, XXI (Feb., 1956), 13-18.

boy or girl. Like the typical family, this primary group also appears highly disorganized and unstable to an outsider. The rapidity with which gang members come and go and the loose connections which bind the often numerous peripheral hangers-on to the tiny nuclear group are largely an accommodation to the local social situation and not an indication of a collapsing institution. High mobility rates, frequency of imprisonment, intense competition for rank, and impaired capacity for sustained personal relationships, related to defective family integration, lie behind this loosely structured type of organization. The fact is that practically every boy and most girls twelve years of age or older strive to gain gang membership. These groups possess a clear-cut structure, with a value system, an inner core of three to four members and an outer circle of from four to eight floaters, a hangout, a strong neighbourhood identification, flexible rules of meeting, and their own codes of morality. Moreover, they play a basic role in initiating youngsters into the neighbourhood culture, including early sexual experience, drinking, stealing, passing "hot" goods, and learning how to "live it up" on good days without being dismayed at the thought of what tomorrow may bring. Lower Ward gangs assist members in learning codes governing loyalty, self-respect, and competition and the rules for acceptance of ethnic groups, besides conveying some sense of belonging to a group and to a neighbourhood. They also teach adolescents how to participate simultaneously and with ease in both the legitimate larger society and the delinquent world of the slum. Such acculturation to a dichotomous culture is essential to later adult adjustment to life in the lower Ward.

The teen-age gang is an integral part of the lower Ward "old Canadian" social system. Its popularity and appeal is closely related to a situation of congested living and weak family controls and to parental absenteeism or harshness which fosters a sharp break between teen-agers and their parents. Early leaving of school and the need for status in a pre-adult world and for support in breaking with parental restrictions and controls foster gang development. In the lower Ward, gangs are strongly neighbourhood-focussed. They tend to draw their members from a small area, "hang out" in local Queen Street restaurants, and "pull" their jobs within the district. However, through trips to cheap dance halls and settlement houses outside the area they meet other teen-agers from fairly distant areas and partnerships become established which introduce lower Ward adolescents to an enlarged community but one still dominated by low status codes and standards.

Among housewives, the formation of close relationships with one or two neighbours constitutes another type of primary group association. Residential mobility is a constant threat to such relationships, although many are strong enough to survive moves to east-end lower-class districts. In the representative sample interviewed, 60 per cent admitted to at least one close neighbourhood friendship. Frequently this was with a next-door neighbour or the housewife in the other half of the subdivided house. On some streets a friendship group numbering three or four housewives meets daily for coffee. Other housewife friendships are built around meetings at the local beer parlour, usually between two and four o'clock in the afternoon. Not infrequently these neighbourhood friendship relationships are strained by serious quarrels, and regroupings, temporary or permanent, occur. As one school principal observed, "Living in small *cul-de-sacs*, or cut off by factories or parking lots, it is natural that their relationships will be intense and demonstrate a constant on-again, off-again pattern."

This neighbourhood pattern is associated with a considerable amount of gossip and knowledge of each other's business. Personal relationships become all important, especially in the dead-end or broken streets where the population of the immediate neighbourhood may total only twelve families. Long-established families—and every street has a few which have lived in the same house for ten to twenty years—often act as a focus for this neighbourhood "knowing." Here, too, neighbourhood stores, which dot the lower Ward practically one to every block, facilitate the regular meeting of close neighbours and strengthen their identification with the locality by providing a convenient centre for gossip and socializing. This is inevitably more characteristic of social life in the more easterly parts of the area where grocery shops tend to be managed by Anglo-Saxons than in the western sections where new Canadians dominate the corner-store business, but even here a great deal of "social" shopping goes on, helping to strengthen identification of new Canadians with the lower Ward district.

Women's friendship ties also tend to be related to certain church groups such as the mothers' meeting or mothers' club, and to Roman Catholic sponsored bingo games. Most of the non-Roman Catholic churches have one or two such groups for local "old Canadians" whose programme is almost entirely social and where old friendships are maintained and occasionally broadened. (These clubs are only nominally formal organizations; their strength lies not in the church connection or the formal structure, which is usually very loose, but in the ease with which they accommodate the primary group friendship interests of their membership.) Again, a sizeable percentage of the housewives, especially those without husbands or married to quiet, unsociable men, commonly attended bingoes in or near the lower Ward every week. Since 1958, however, Roman Catholic churches have discontinued bingoes in the vicinity of the lower Ward, and this occasion for renewing friendship ties, in an exciting atmosphere, no longer exists.

Relationships arising out of work or pub associations rather than out of physical proximity on the street dominate the men's social world. Primary group ties predominate here too. Very few men actively participate in churches or unions, although some, usually the older ones, belong to veterans' clubs, two of which are located in the area. These last, however, like church mothers' clubs, can hardly be classified as formal associations, since they make their appeal principally on the basis of offering cheaper beer and better facilities for playing cards than the pub.

It is the beer parlour, or the pub as it is commonly called, that dominates the social life of the lower Ward "old Canadian" men.[26] Of the seventeen drinking establishments in the area, fourteen (three along King and eleven along Queen Street) are centres for neighbourhood social activity. Four of these are modern and attractive in design, having a cocktail bar and dining room and beverage rooms seating 200 to 300 persons. Almost all the others are plain to run-down in appearance, and small in size, accommodating from forty to seventy persons a piece in the men's and ladies' rooms. The total capacity of all seventeen establishments is approximately 1,800.[27]

Open from noon to six and from eight to midnight,[28] these pubs daily serve a changing clientele of "regulars" plus casual visitors. The first group of "regulars" crowding in just after noon consists largely of nearby office and factory workers and truckers, some of whom bring a sandwich while others buy a light lunch. The four equipped with dining room and cocktail bar serve a popular business men's luncheon. Around 1:30 p.m., a new group enters, principally "old-timers," including pensioners, unemployables, and men retired or on workmen's compensation. These non-workers usually sit towards the rear and gossip idly for hours over a few beers. At

[26] This is almost equally true of the older, new Canadians in the area.
[27] All but two of the fourteen have ladies' rooms.
[28] Those with cocktail bars remain open later.

3 o'clock, housewives will begin to fill up the ladies' room, staying till 4:30 or 5 o'clock. Between 4 and 4:30, office and factory workers, truckers, and other workers flood in for the after-work beer and chat. Most chairs will be taken. In the evening, another group of largely local residents—except in the four establishments with cocktail bars—pours in. Thursdays to Saturdays all fourteen beverage rooms will be well filled between 9:30 and 11:00 p.m.[29] After eleven some leave, while the after-show group will fill up the bigger places; a small group will remain till midnight, and move to the cocktail bar or dining room, staying until the last possible moment. This general pattern is not confined to Toronto's lower Ward.[30]

With the partial exception of the four selling cocktails, all fourteen pubs in the lower Ward draw largely from the immediate neighbourhood. Thus, one attracts its customers from a radius of about three blocks to east, west, south and north; another from one block east, four west, and three south. Certain ones draw heavily from one or two ethnic groups; for example, one caters to Finns, one to central Europeans, others to "old Canadians." Specialization also occurs to some extent in terms of gambling "facilities" or social levels; a few have restrictive standards of acceptability while several have almost no standards at all. Interviews of our population sample and other evidence suggest that 70 to 80 per cent of the men have one or two favourite pubs and patronize these at least twice a week.

In spite of certain distinctions, all fourteen pubs seemed to possess a common culture, atmosphere, and web of social functions. The culture is characterized by lower-class standards of furnishings, dress, manners, and language, directness of personal interaction, a strong interest in sports (especially boxing and wrestling), sex, and drinking, and a concentration on informal, primary group, particularistic relationships. A noisy, permissive atmosphere, bordering occasionally on license and simulating the freedom of the working man's living room, is also characteristic. A man may read, sleep with head on table, stare at the wall, swear noisily, get into a fight, talk with a stranger, begin and cease conversation at will. A fundamental norm is open acceptance of both idiosyncrasies of behaviour and moral outlook and different social types and races. Thus, the handicapped, the man with no roof in his mouth, the half-breed, the negro, the wino and transient, the prostitute, either pretty or emaciated, the

[29] Except when the Woodbine race track is open; then they are half empty.
[30] See D. Gottlieb, "The Neighbourhood Tavern and the Cocktail Lounge," *American Journal of Sociology*, LXII (May, 1957).

homosexual, pimp, or gambler are all accepted without stares or other forms of social ostracism. However, most managers try to enforce a code against excessive drinking or fighting, according to their respective standards.

In social function, the pubs act as working men's social clubs, with slight variations in atmosphere and rules but with a common orientation. Here is how one observant resident of the area puts it:

I believe the pubs have real social functions; they are the poor man's club, the equivalent of the rich man's Granite Club. They're treated well there. Going there may help solve problems, domestic or job difficulties. Also they get a sense of importance there, perhaps in ordering the beer, or showing off in talk with the guys. They do band together to meet emergencies, for instance sickness. . . . The poor have to find people on their level; this is so, in the pub. . . . The pub keeper has high status. . . . He is well fixed financially, but it takes a lot of work. He treats the clientele with kindness; they have to learn how to treat their people well, and some are difficult to handle.

Within the normal functioning of the working man's club, certain needs of the whole male population and of specific groups within it are met. In the absence of any neighbourhood recreational or cultural centre for "old Canadians," the pub serves as the neighbourhood or community centre. Here one meets practically the whole neighbourhood group, especially on Fridays and Saturdays, learns the latest gossip, and identifies with the neighbourhood. This is also the place where the two worlds of legitimate society and underworld come together, in an acceptable, convenient form. Here one can dispose of or buy "hot" goods, either openly through a waiter or in the washroom, place a bet,[31] "pick up" a woman, or get the particulars on a "blind pig." On the other hand, one can participate freely in the legitimate male world, talk about sports, sex, work, unions or even politics.[32] In the absence of other facilities for male recreation, it provides a recreational service, in permitting animated conversation, watching of television, and participation in gambling through bookies. Socially, it is "the place to go" and within its nexus of primary group relationships the individual finds his locus and social standing. He sits with his buddies, demonstrates his degree of technical knowledge (for example, of truck driving) and of social information, exchanges jokes with waiters and old-timers, and in these and similar subtle ways validates his belonging to and status

[31] Banks of telephones in the hotel lobby make it easy for bookies to report bets.
[32] One publican, however, has a rule that politics must not be discussed, as he believes it leads to too many fights.

within the neighbourhood group. Thus, in the almost complete absence of effective participation in formal associations, the pub community secures a sense of integration and conveys a sense of status to its regulars. Certain pub groups, particularly those gathering at regular hours almost every day, tend to resemble the extended family in the freedom, depth, and intimacy of their interrelations. Moreover, for people of the lower Ward, as one informant put it, "the pub gives them a release from pressures, restrictions, crowdedness, and drabness, and some kind of real lift."

Within the pub, the publican or manager tends to play the role of head of the household, endeavouring to maintain the harmony and integration of the group, and the goodwill of all patrons. Although a strong pecuniary interest is not absent, a number of these men become deeply involved in the individual personalities and problems of their "regulars." An extended family-like structure seems to emerge, where the beverage room appears to function as an enlarged "living room" and the pub society in effect compensates for the weakness of family and kin relationships among the male group. In sharp contrast with cramped smelly living quarters at home, the ladies' beverage room offers both husband and wife a pleasant setting removed from the incessant demands of young children.

Whereas housewives tend to gain social support from particular kin members, such as mothers, sisters, or brothers, many men become dependent upon their pub buddies. Pub regulars support their drinking buddies in various ways. They may offer free drinks when a man is broke, loans of money until next pay-day, rough and ready advice on marital or occupational problems as well as companionship in hours of anger, trouble, or perplexity. In addition, they may organize collections to help with financial emergencies or to send flowers to a buddy confined in a hospital. Aggressive urges resulting in verbal battles or fist fights may also find release within such an accepting group which functions, in co-operation with the publican, to shield the offending party from the police. As one pub keeper pointed out:

We have one or two fights a week. . . . We try to avoid calling in the police. For one thing it has complications. A report goes from the police to the Liquor Commission; an inspector comes around to ask questions, and fills out a form. Too many fights and we may be asked to close up for a week or two.

The publican, who is called by his first name or "Pop" and often acts as a father surrogate, plays many roles: he gives advice on legal or medical problems, provides aid in finding a job or offers a job recommendation, helps fill out legal documents including income tax forms, cashes cheques, large or small, makes loans of money (in one pub, for instance, they have a floating fund of $100 for such loans to regulars), sends flowers to patrons ill in the hospital, helps with their hospital or funeral expenses, and even serves as a pall-bearer. In addition, he provides information on deviant activities, gambling, bookmaking, bootlegging, prostitution, and such, and in general gives the impression that, like the father of a family, he stands ready to help with any reasonable—and many unreasonable—requests.

The pub plays a crucial supporting role for certain specific groups. Perhaps the most important of these are the single men, particularly those who rent accommodation in rooms above the beer parlour. Almost all of the ten smaller establishments have ten to twenty such rooms to rent and let out about 50 per cent of these to "regulars." For these men the beer parlour is precisely their living room and the publican their "grand-daddy." Thus, one of the more responsible pub keepers observed:

We look after our roomers if they get sick. . . . Some of them have been here twenty years, and quite a few ten years. Especially on Sunday morning, a beer before breakfast goes very good and so we let them have one. The law says you can't serve beer in the rooms, but that's one law I don't observe.

These hotel residents, besides hundreds of other single men trapped in tiny single rooms in the area, often without a radio, find in the beer parlour an informal home-like atmosphere, friendship, and entertainment in the television set—much of which is unavailable elsewhere.[33] Some virtually *live* in the beer parlour, stretching out a beer for an hour or picking up free drinks from a stream of friends.

The pub also functions as a sort of home for the winos, of which it is conservatively estimated there are upwards of 200 in the area. These alcoholics scheme incessantly how to secure the next 10 cents for a glass of beer or 25 cents towards a bottle of cheap wine,[34] and customarily hang around certain pubs looking for treats or hand-outs. The pub is also the most convenient place where such drunks may get cleaned up, or in cold weather find temporary shelter and warmth. Although practically all pub keepers try to keep out the worst winos, these unfortunates constantly think up new ways to get in and work their "angles." The fact is that not only will no other

[33] The churches have nothing resembling a club or social programme for such men.
[34] With 25 cents they can, with the help of a buddy, soon make up the 75 cents for a bottle.

place have them[35] but the pub is the only society in which they can feel at home. So, for this group, the beer parlour functions as home and also as base of operations. Professional deviants such as book-makers, bootleggers, and prostitutes likewise use the pub as a convenient base, and, of course, the latter meet their assignations "upstairs."[36] One publican intimated, "I know eight bootleggers personally...they don't hide it. They come here frequently."

Specific functions are also performed for old age pensioners, the unemployed, nearby workers, newcomers to the area, and the lonely. Pensioners and the unemployed, with so little to do around the house or in the area, pass away the time and gain acceptance within a group of their fellows at the pub. Nearby factory and office workers who flood in at noon or after work find the beer parlour a congenial restaurant, whose facilities are often superior in relaxation, entertainment, and conversation to those of most nearby grills. Newcomers to the area and those who are afflicted by pangs of loneliness find conversations are easy to strike up and drinking friends easy to make. In an area where mobility and social isolation rates are high, this function is not unimportant.

The lower Ward's hotel-pubs thus function to meet many community and subgroup needs. They also facilitate the simultaneous participation of residents in both the illegitimate and the conventional value system. Certain drinking establishments located at strategic corners, particularly the corner of Bathurst and Queen streets, equipped with dining room and cocktail bar, provide opportunities for participation in a wide range of conventional and illegitimate activities. The presence of a nearby complex of institutions including a wine store, a brewer's outlet, several all-night grills, a movie house, a steam bath—where homosexuals congregate—a brothel, and several smoke shops and drug stores enriches the variety of both deviant and legitimate services and makes this corner the focus for recreation, entertainment, companionship, and deviant services for much of the area west of Spadina, and also an acceptable meeting ground between the lower Ward and the surrounding urban community. In particular, seekers of deviant services from working- and middle-class areas invade the lower Ward in greatest numbers at this busy intersection and help perpetuate its Toronto-wide notoriety. Among deviant activities, gambling, bookmaking, prostitution, pro-

[35] The church missions usually feed them and then force them outside.
[36] Some hotels have special rates for one or two hours, to accommodate the prostitute trade.

miscuity, homosexuality, fencing, bootlegging, thievery, and plotting of crime are all prominent around the corner. As one resident commented: "There are a thousand ways around here to get your mind off things." This is not to minimize these activities throughout the whole lower Ward, for instance, bootlegging, which is carried on in one or more houses in nearly every residential block of the area, but simply to note their point of concentration.

The extensiveness of institutionalized and spasmodic illegitimate activity is associated with basic economic, social, and characterological tendencies in the area of the lower Ward. Certain illegitimate businesses, for instance bookmaking or bootlegging, may be started by "amateurs" simply as means of increasing an unsatisfactory income. While many bootleggers and some bookies carry on in a part-time amateur fashion, others quickly shift into full-time operations. The local demand for bootlegging, given the popularity of drinking, the large number of compulsory drinkers, and Liquor Commission closing regulations at night and on Sundays[37] is high. The appeal of gambling to both old and new Canadians, and the formidable difficulties of getting to the racetrack makes for a steady demand. One elderly, knowledgeable informant[38] claimed that bookmaking is the biggest business in Toronto. A high police official stated there are probably two hundred "back rooms" in the city, many of which would be in the lower Ward. The protest character of this activity and its promise of financial gain inevitably make it popular. Likewise, fencing is a natural concomitant of the local pattern of petty thievery, the low income of most residents with the consequent interest in "bargain" prices, and the lack of condemnation of such an activity in the local mores. Its characteristic informal, unorganized form and concentration in the beer parlours simply indicates an adjustment to the larger social system of the area.

The Mertonian thesis that deviant activities are related to dissociation of cultural goals and institutional means is generally illuminating for our area. While participation in illegitimate activities often represents an attempt to compensate for exclusion from middle-class goal achievement, in other cases it also represents a means to acquire a livelihood (as prostitute or bookie) or to augment what is earned in more legitimate channels.[39] Another type of reaction to

[37] Sunday is the big day for local bootleggers.
[38] This gentleman, who has lived in the area for thirty-five years, although formally identified with legitimate church work, had many underworld connections in the area.
[39] The janitor at one large local church operated as a bookie on the side.

goals-means dissociation is that of listless apathy, represented in this area by numerous individuals for whom television is the only source of recreation and entertainment. This is common among isolated women and some men, especially those with no pub or neighbourhood connections.

In accounting for deviant behaviour, Cloward has pointed out the significance of opportunities to acquire the illegitimate skills and values and to discharge and practise them.[40] While opportunities to learn petty thievery, gambling, bootlegging, and bookmaking are not lacking in the lower Ward, apparently few organized criminal gangs exist to train young men in big crimes, such as is common in some large American cities. Apart from one or two criminal "mobs" who move their headquarters from place to place along Queen Street, especially vicious or highly organized criminals are not attached to the lower Ward. Something of this type of crime seems to be found perhaps a half mile to the north, where big gambling clubs function along with dope rings[41] and more highly organized prostitution. Thus, a lack of the requisite institutions and the organized adult mob which trains men in big crime, along with the general bent of the lower Ward's social system which emphasizes small primary group activity, militates against the emergence of powerful criminal mobs or machines.

Illegal and immoral practices are, however, thoroughly meshed with the legitimate and conventional social patterns in the lower Ward. While the police usually wink at bootlegging[42] and make only spasmodic efforts to stamp out such habits as gambling, prostitution, and fencing, school, church, and social work functionaries eschew any systematic efforts to investigate or expose such practices and business men along Queen Street maintain, in general, a discreet silence. Each important element in the indigenous social system— family, neighbourhood group, teen-age gang, and pub community— is tied in directly, or by a conspiracy of silence, with the deviant social structure. This is inevitable, for what the authorities "up there" label as delinquent or immoral or illegitimate is frequently an adjustment to the peculiar socio-economic conditions of the district, and meets important needs of the community or subgroups within it.

[40] Richard A. Cloward, "Illegimate Means, Anomie and Deviant Behaviour," *American Sociological Review* (April, 1959), 167-9.
[41] It appears that taking dope is fundamentally against the mores among the main "old Canadian" group in the lower Ward.
[42] If the police were to arrest all bootleggers in the lower Ward and elsewhere in Toronto, the jails would be full to overflowing, and there would be an impossible congestion in the magistrates' courts.

The
Urban Community and
Changing Moral Standards

J. R. BURNET

TWO CONTRARY ASSUMPTIONS about sobriety and piety dwell comfortably side by side. On the one hand, they are considered, like thrift and industry, as characteristics of the country rather than the city. The freedom, diversity, anonymity, and excitement of urban life are thought to encourage hedonism, while the rural pattern of living, with its stress on hard work, strong informal social controls, and lack of opportunity for dissipation, is believed conducive to self-denial and restraint. In Canada the surveys of the Canadian Institute of Public Opinion dealing with attitudes towards Sunday observance and the drinking of alcoholic beverages substantiate this view. On the other hand, qualities such as sobriety have been linked with the Protestant ethic, and hence with urbanism and capitalism; their exercise in one's own calling and their imposition on others are considered to have played a part in providing the modern entrepreneur with a clear conscience and a disciplined work-force.

The reputation of many large cities for strictness in moral matters bears witness to the fact that urbanism does not preclude puritanism. Canadian cities generally have had such a reputation, and Toronto in particular has been regarded as the quintessence of severity. It has been looked upon as suspicious of amusements, hostile to the arts, censorious of any but religious activities outside the home on the Lord's Day, and opposed to the drinking of alcoholic beverages and therefore concerned with making liquor hard to get and the facilities for public drinking few and repellent.[1] Even now, when its streets flaunt the neon signs of cocktail lounges and taverns and crowds of sports enthusiasts and concert-goers break its Sunday hush, it has not lost its nickname "the Good."

[1] A witty satire on Toronto and its reputation is Lister Sinclair's "We All Hate Toronto" in *A Play on Words and Other Radio Plays* (Toronto, 1948).

Toronto's ethos and reputation were shaped in the 1830's and 1840's by the upward thrust of business men and industrialists in a town previously dominated by aristocratic groups. The members of the rising middle class had a puritanical morality which they impressed on the community, and long after their sons and grandsons had adopted less rigid standards its stamp endured. But after more than a hundred years a new middle-class morality, developed in a more urban, industrial, and bureaucratic society, is beginning to efface the old.

The temperance and sabbatarian movements in their advance and retreat tell much of the story of Toronto puritanism. The two movements were closely akin. They arose at the same time; they drew support and opposition from virtually the same sections of the population; although temperance was more highly organized, they underwent similar changes in structure and aim; and they are now declining together.

When the temperance movement began its sweep through British North America in the late 1820's and the 1830's, Montreal rather than Toronto was the temperance capital of the Canadas, of which it was also the brewing and distilling centre. John Dougall, a Scottish merchant with interests in both Upper and Lower Canada, sparked a vast number of activities. Notably, he and his fellow members of the Montreal Temperance Society sent out agents to hold meetings and found societies, and from 1835 on they published a journal of exceptional longevity, the *Canada Temperance Advocate*.

In Toronto vigorous action began later. "Perhaps in no place in Canada," said the *Christian Guardian*, "has prejudice been so obstinate and inveterate against Temperance Societies as in this town."[2] A society was formed in 1830, expressly as a central organization for the province, and began an ambitious fact-finding project, but it soon languished. It revived in 1833 and presumably took part in arranging the Provincial Temperance Convention held in Toronto in 1836, but died in the following year. There was also a Toronto Young Men's Temperance Society, which in 1835 changed its name to the Toronto Temperance Society. The *Temperance Record*, a journal published by Jesse Ketchum and others, ended its short career in 1837. The Rebellion was disturbing to the temperance cause: John Dougall included political division among the reasons for the thin attendance at a temperance meeting in Toronto in 1838.[3]

[2] Nov. 20, 1830.
[3] *Canada Temperance Advocate*, April, 1838.

However, by 1839 a hardy organization, the Temperance Reformation Society of the City of Toronto, was in existence, and it quickly took over some of the tasks in which Montreal had pioneered.

The temperance societies pledged individuals to voluntary abstention, from ardent spirits at first and later from fermented liquors as well. Their meetings, open to all, featured speeches by clergymen and noted temperance orators. Often the entertainment was augmented by heckling and other demonstrations of hostility from drunkards, tavern keepers, distillers, or brewers. Sometimes those who came to jeer were among the pledge-signers at the meeting's end, to the edification and pleasure of the assembly.

At the time, self-restraint was also the aim of the sabbatarian movement which had as its object the enforcement of idleness on Sunday and the hedging of it stoutly against indulgence. In this case, however, fewer societes were founded to strengthen individuals in their resolves. Activities frowned upon included working or requiring others to work; lying late in bed; reading novels, romance, or politics; engaging in "idle ramblings of recreation"—hunting, fishing, and visiting; travelling, and especially going with groups of acquaintances on pleasure excursions on Sunday.[4] Accidental deaths were described as the fruits of Sabbath-breaking.[5] The example of a coloured hairdresser who gave notice that he would do no business on the Sabbath was commended to others.[6]

The drinking customs in Toronto at the time of the rise of the temperance movement have been sketched by Pearson:

The custom of drinking intoxicating liquor was very general and a large majority of the people used either spirits (generally whiskey), beer or wines at the dinner table. Even among the Methodists (principally those from the Old Country), who were supposed to be teetotalers, the use of beer as a beverage was quite common. In fact, Messrs. John Doel, Joseph Bloor, and George Rowell, all Methodists, were brewers.

Treating was very common. Instead of tipping a cabman or the driver of a stage, he was usually treated. It was not generally considered disreputable for a gentleman to get drunk after dinner. The custom of men making New Year's Day calls was very general. With refreshments wine was usually served and sometimes stronger beverages, and it was not an uncommon sight to see men reeling through the streets and sometimes uproariously drunk at the close of the day. The physiological effect of alcohol was not then understood, and it was generally thought healthful to take a little wine, beer, or spirits, and the use of

[4] *Christian Guardian, passim.* See especially Oct. 15, 1831, and Dec. 8, 1841.
[5] *Ibid.,* Aug. 3, 1836, and May 9, 1838.
[6] *Ibid.,* Nov. 10, 1841.

alcoholic beverages was much more freely recommended by the physician of the time than it is today.[7]

In 1845 Toronto was described as a large, bustling, cheerful, and wealthy city, but a sad drunken place in need of a Father Mathew,[8] and in the following year as a famous place for drinking and drunkenness.[9]

In the eyes of the Rev. William Proudfoot, a staunch Scottish sabbatarian, the town observed Sunday inadequately. On October 7, 1832, he recorded in his diary, "There seems to be a good deal of church-going at York, and also a great deal of carelessness and Sabbath desecration. Things are done openly here which I never saw done in Scotland...." The following spring, on Good Friday, he wrote:

The town was much more quiet than on Sabbath last. The reason I suppose is, that on the Sabbath many who do not care for religion, yet dare not outrage public feeling as to work or shoot in the woods, and therefore lounge about the streets, and being idle they become disorderly, but on a holiday they get out and amuse themselves in the way they best can, and therefore there is more of public decency in the appearance of the town on a holiday than on a Sabbath. The Canadians besides like a play day at any time but they grudge the observance of the Sabbath.[10]

The Toronto supporters of the moral reform movements in the 1830's and 1840's seem to have been several thousand strong, while the city's population was rising from about ten to twenty-five thousand. They were predominantly middle class; Methodist, Baptist, Congregationalist, and, especially in the sabbatarian cause, Presbyterian; American and Scottish in ethnic background; and Reform in politics. Jesse Ketchum, "the father of temperance in Toronto"[11] and an ardent and generous supporter of Sunday Schools, was outstanding but not unrepresentative: a tanner who in spite of his wealth and philanthropy was not accepted in the best society, an American who retained strong ties with his homeland and eventually returned to it, a Reformer. He was an Anglican, but his benefactions went to several denominations.[12]

[7] W. H. Pearson, *Recollections and Records of Toronto of Old* (Toronto, 1914), pp. 233-4.
[8] Rubio (Thomas Horton James), *Rambles in the United States and Canada during the Year 1845* (London, 1846), pp. 96-7.
[9] *Christian Guardian*, March 25, 1846.
[10] The Proudfoot Papers, *Transactions*, London and Middlesex Historical Society, VI (1918), 45, and *Papers and Records*, Ontario Historical Society, XXVI (1930), 522.
[11] *Globe*, March 30, 1860.
[12] E. J. Hathaway, *Jesse Ketchum and His Times* (Toronto, 1929), p. 136.

The movements did not make much progress among the lower classes, and the *Christian Guardian,* the *Globe,* and other journals espousing moral reform frequently lamented the lack of leadership and even opposition from those in high places. On April 4, 1832, the *Christian Guardian* suggested that one reason why so few of the official and leading men of the province came forward in the cause of temperance might be that other, presumably humbler, persons had been first to introduce temperance societies. A few months later it complained that Upper Canada was the only part of British America where the social leaders did not assist in promoting temperance societies.[13] James Silk Buckingham, on a lecture tour in 1840, wrote of Toronto:

There is a Temperance Society here, on the principle of total abstinence from all that can intoxicate, but their numbers are few, the higher classes of society, and the Episcopal clergy, withholding their patronage and support. During one of the evenings of my stay here, I delivered a public address on the subject of Temperance in the Wesleyan Methodist Church, but though it was very numerously attended, there were very few of the leading families among the auditory; and the only members of the clergy present were a Congregational minister and a Roman Catholic priest. The absence of all the heads of the community on this occasion could not be attributed to any other cause than their indifference or unwillingness to countenance or uphold the Temperance cause; for when my lectures on Egypt and Palestine were given in the same building, one course before and the other after the Temperance address, the church was crowded to excess and there was scarcely a family of any note or influence absent.[14]

The Toronto *Gazette* also commented on the absence of "judicial and literary characters" at Buckingham's temperance lecture.[15]

The middle class is the great breeding ground of reform movements. When the temperance movement arose in the United States, however, in the last years of the eighteenth century, its leaders were said to be "the rich, the well-born, and the able."[16] These men conceived of the movement as a philanthropic endeavour which might shore up the aristocratic position against the flood-tides of change; but when it became a moral crusade, under the impact of revivalism and Jacksonian democracy, some of them remained leaders in it.[17]

[13] Dec. 26, 1832.

[14] *Canada, Nova Scotia, New Brunswick* (London, 1843), pp. 25-7.

[15] *Journal of the American Temperance Union,* Sept., 1840.

[16] Krout, *The Origins of Prohibition* (New York, 1925), p. 92.

[17] By the 1830's the upper classes in the United States held aloof. Cf. the dialogue in the *Canada Temperance Advocate* of September 1836, and "Well Enough for the Vulgar" and "Do They Not Need It?" in the *Journal of the American Temperance Union,* Jan., 1837.

In Toronto, on the other hand, the social leaders, owing their position to tradition, regarded traditional restraints as adequate to prevent alcoholic (and other) excesses.

Of religious groups the Methodists were the most active in moral reform. To them intemperance was sin. It did not matter overmuch what casuists could make of biblical texts about wine and strong drink: drunkenness was evil, and avoiding it was one of the fruits of repentance by which alone one could recognize entrance upon a new life. By 1840 at the latest, total abstinence was an integral part of Methodism. It was said that each Methodist church was a temperance society, but the members and the clergy also joined the specifically temperance associations in order to reinforce their pledges and set an example to others. Egerton Ryerson was secretary of the first York (Toronto) temperance society, and the journal of which he was the first and most influential editor, the *Christian Guardian*, during the thirties ardently advocated temperance and temperance societies. The hardening of the movement can be seen in the disappearance from the *Guardian*'s columns of advertisements for foreign wines and liquors and for reliable brewers, and of recipes for good ale, and in the extension of condemnation from those who drank to those who made and sold beer and spirits. All in all, the pronouncement of the editor of the *Canada Temperance Advocate* that "the Wesleyan Methodists have done more for the Temperance Reformation in Upper Canada than perhaps all other denominations put together" is hard to dispute, and other Methodist bodies did not lag far behind.[18]

Desecration of the Sabbath was also sinful according to Methodism, and the *Christian Guardian* printed cautionary accounts of absentees from church and Sunday school or other Sabbath-breakers who had grave or fatal accidents, as well as of drunkards who came to untimely ends. Not simply abstention from work on Sunday was required but the devotion of the whole of this day and part of Saturday as well to religious duties.

The Presbyterians were less concerned and less united than the Methodists about temperance. Many Scottish Presbyterian ministers were at most lukewarm in their support, and one located near Toronto, the Rev. R. Murrary of Oakville, wrote in 1839 a widely publicized anti-temperance tract, *A Course of Lectures on Absolute*

---

[18] *Christian Guardian*, Sept. 8, 1841. The Methodist Episcopal rather than the British Wesleyan group within the Wesleyan Methodist Church had earned this judgment.

Abstinence.[19] But a few clergymen, especially those of American and Canadian birth, and some laymen were active and enthusiastic temperance workers, and by 1841 the Assembly of the Presbyterian Church of Canada pronounced strongly against intemperance.[20]

Sabbath observance, however, was a prime concern among Presbyterians. The outstanding leader of the sabbatarian cause was the Rev. Dr. Burns of the Free Church who occupied pulpits in Toronto, Kingston, and St. Catharines during the 1840's and 1850's. The Browns of the *Globe* were interested and active, and many of the writers of letters to their newspaper identified themselves as Presbyterians.

The Baptists[21] and Congregationalists also were puritanical in their attitudes to the drinking of alcoholic beverages and the observance of Sunday as a holy day, and supported moral reform. A Congregational minister in Toronto, John Roaf, gave conspicuous leadership in both the temperance and Sabbath observance movements. The Congregationalists were less disturbed by the Rebellion of 1837 than other groups, for the *Canada Temperance Advocate* of June, 1838, noted that whereas in Toronto generally few people could be got to unite for any object, the Congregationalists showed signs of vitality and intended to form a Congregational Temperance Association. The *Advocate* recorded in September, 1841, that the Congregational Union of Upper Canada, meeting at Toronto, had passed a strong resolution recommending total abstinence, and in the following month that all sixteen Congregational ministers in Upper Canada were staunchly teetotal and the Academy for training Congregational ministers thoroughly imbued with teetotal principles.

Anglicanism and Roman Catholicism opposed the moral reform movement, although not unanimously. Though they were against drunkenness, they distrusted total abstinence and temperance societies, and they favoured "the holy hilarity of the Lord's Day" rather than "Jewish severity."[22] According to a correspondent of the *Christian Guardian*, in 1841 the Church of England newspaper went so far as to declare membership in a temperance society inconsistent

---

[19] The Rev. Mr. Murray was shortly afterwards put in charge of the common schools of the province, preceding the great moulder of the school system, Egerton Ryerson.
[20] *Canada Temperance Advocate*, Aug., 1841.
[21] Cf. the *Canadian Baptist Magazine and Missionary Register*, IV (Sept., 1840), p. 52. The founder of the first temperance society in Upper Canada, an American-born physician, Dr. Peter Schofield, was a Baptist.
[22] *Globe*, June 26, 1856.

with membership in the Church of England.[23] Some of the clergy took a stricter stand than the official bodies or the majority of church members, however. A temperance society was established by Toronto Roman Catholics in 1847 with Father Kirwin as president, and continued under Father Fitzhenry; by 1852 it had over two thousand members.[24]

An argument used in British North America against temperance societies was that they might become dangerous political instruments. "In the hands of clever leaders, and designing men, may not a society of this kind become a great political engine?" asked Major Strickland;[25] and Col. Thomas Talbot spoke of black sheep or rebels who "commenced their work of darkness under the cover of organizing Damned Cold Water Drinking Societies, where they meet at night to communicate their poisonous and seditious schemes to each other and to devise the best mode of circulating the infection, so as to impose upon and delude the simple and unwary."[26] In Toronto, those advocating reform displayed two characteristics to occasion such fears: they were predominantly American and to a lesser degree Scottish, and their leaders in the 1830's included such prominent Reformers as Jesse Ketchum, Thomas Stoyell, John Rolph, and Marshall Spring Bidwell.

As in social class so in the ethnic and political affiliations of its adherents, temperance in Toronto lacked one of the claims to respectability that it flaunted in the United States. There the movement was native. It had grown up in the United States; it was consonant with American institutions; its leaders were mainly "old Americans." Its enemies from an early date were identified with foreign influences and Roman Catholicism.[27] In British North America, since national pride was of much slower growth, the same claim, even if it could have been made, would have been less effective. The Canadian movement, however, was patently tied to that of the United States; indeed, it was an integral part of a general movement of temperance, neither Canadian nor American, but having its centre in the more populous and highly developed country.

[23] July 28, 1841.
[24] Canadian Son of Temperance and Literary Gem, Jan. 14, 1852.
[25] Major S. Strickland, Twenty-seven Years in Canada West; or, The Experience of an Early Settler (London, 1853), p. 142.
[26] C. O. Ermatinger, The Talbot Regime or the First Half Century of the Talbot Settlement (St. Thomas, 1904), p. 167.
[27] In the 1830's the anti-temperance crusader, Calvin Colton, claimed that the movement attacked the liberties of the American people, but subversion was a difficult charge to maintain.

When the temperance societies had gathered in substantial sections of the population, new techniques were tried to reach the still unconverted. The societies began to enlist female and juvenile support and to organize musical bands; in Toronto they set up ward committees to hold meetings to convert working men to the cause and confirm them in it. Secret societies also grew up, apparently as a result of the failure of the Washingtonian movement in the United States and of its counterpart the Victoria Temperance Society movement in the Canadas. Such societies arose among reformed drunkards rather than the respectable and represented attempts to exert stronger controls over converts than the open societies could. The most prominent were the Order of the Sons of Temperance which entered the Canadas from the United States about 1848 and reached its peak in 1852, and the Independent Order of Good Templars which was brought into the Canadas in 1855 and soon outshone the Sons. Both were benefit societies; both had passwords, regalia, elaborate hierarchies of pompously-titled officers; but whereas women might join the Good Templars, for many years they were relegated to the Daughters of Temperance and kept separate from the Sons. Finally, in 1853 the Canada Temperance League, soon renamed the Canadian Prohibitory Liquor Law League, was set up to embrace all temperance supporters, including individuals who were not teetotal themselves but interested in forwarding temperance legislation.

The foundation of the League followed a change of emphasis from moral suasion to political action. Legislation had never been disdained: the Provincial Temperance Convention of 1836 adopted resolutions in favour of petitioning the legislature to restrict the manufacture and sale of intoxicating liquors, and calling upon the constituted authorities to withhold licences to sell spirituous liquors as far as possible. But in the 1840's the securing of legal restrictions emerged as a dominant objective. Like others elsewhere, Toronto citizens had long been clamouring for municipal regulations reducing the number of liquor licences that should be granted, and for enforcement of the regulations already passed. Licensing was an important source of municipal revenue and also of corruption. Now the city became the headquarters for activity designed to secure provincial prohibitory legislation: the signing of petitions, the holding of processions and demonstrations, the importing of outstanding orators. In October, 1850, and in September, 1852, J. B. Gough, one of the most redoubtable of temperance speakers (and backsliders), gave courses of lectures. On the first occasion he was said to have received fourteen hundred pledges and to have inspired several gentlemen of standing who were engaged in the spirit trade to look upon their business with semi-horror and to express an earnest wish to get out of it.[28]

From 1846 on, the agitation was directed towards securing a Maine Law.[29] Several times it seemed within reach: in 1855 its opponents resorted to a technicality to defeat it. Thereafter popular excitement declined, but in 1859 a law was secured closing liquor shops and saloons in Canada West from seven o'clock Saturday night to eight o'clock Monday morning, and in 1864 a major success was attained with the passing of the Dunkin Act. This gave counties, cities, towns, townships, and villages in Ontario and Quebec the authority to prohibit by popular vote the retail sale of liquor within their limits.[30] A renewed surge of temperance fervour in the early 1870's resulted during this decade in the formation of the Dominion Alliance for the Total Suppression of the Liquor Traffic (1876), the transformation of the Ontario Temperance and Prohibitory League into the Ontario Branch of the Alliance (1877), and the passing of the Canada Temperance Act or Scott Act (1878), making local option available for cities and counties and applicable throughout Canada. The same wave brought the Women's Christian Temperance Union into active life: in Toronto it made representations to the Council in 1876 which led to a reduction in the number of tavern and shop licences and an increase in the licence fee.

In 1876 the Crooks Act was carried through the Ontario legislature. This act entrusted the granting of licences to a board of responsible men appointed by the government for each riding, and limited the number of licences granted. It was made more stringent over the years by amendments. The Baptist business man, William Davies, wrote from Toronto that the Act very much circumscribed the sale of liquor and occasioned a tempest among those deprived of their licences as well as among brewers and others.[31]

Davies believed that public opinion would not be ready for prohibition "in this generation," and his view was substantiated when Toronto failed to come under the Dunkin Act. A vote was taken in August, 1877, a few months after York County had decided in

[28] *Globe*, Oct. 17, Oct. 24, Oct. 26, and Nov. 2, 1850.
[29] The State of Maine passed a highly restrictive liquor law in 1846, and a prohibitory law in 1851.
[30] R. E. Spence, *Prohibition in Canada* (Toronto, 1919), p. 92.
[31] *Letters of William Davies, Toronto, 1854-61*, ed. by W. S. Fox (Toronto, 1945), p. 134.

favour of the Act by a majority of 455 in an aggregate vote of 7,769. The campaign in the city was vigorous. Those opposed to the Act presented petitions signed by some 5,000 citizens asking that no vote be held, and when this move failed they formed an Anti-Dunkin Association which held meetings in a rink on Adelaide Street West. The prohibitionists built an amphitheatre at the corner of Queen and Yonge streets capable of seating several thousand. The voting was open—this was the last open voting in Toronto—and took place in a new drill shed behind the city hall. It lasted from August 6 to August 22, with some intimidation of voters on the first day by the anti-Dunkin forces. The result was 2,947 votes for the Dunkin Act and 4,063 against, and was hailed by a "grand triumphant, Anti-Dunkin torchlight procession," followed by fireworks and balloon ascensions in Queen's Park.

The years 1886 and 1887 had special importance for the temperance and sabbatarian causes in Toronto. Largely because of dissatisfaction over the licensed and unlicensed liquor traffic, an informal Municipal Reform Association put forward W. H. Howland as candidate for mayor. He was elected with a majority of 1,900, and when prevented from taking office because of a technicality he was re-elected. He immediately called for reforms in the administration of the licence law, and by the end of the year reported considerable improvement. His return to office with an increased majority in 1887 emboldened temperance men to submit to the voters proposals for further changes, but at the municipal elections of 1888 these were decisively rejected.[32]

In 1894, after the carrying of a prohibition plebiscite, the temperance forces of the province converged upon Toronto and sent a deputation to Sir Oliver Mowat to urge total prohibition. He was able then as throughout his premiership to withstand the pressure.[33]

Early in 1908 the city council passed a by-law reducing the number of liquor licences that might be issued from 150 to 110. The courts quashed the by-law but agitation continued. A plebiscite was arranged for January, 1909, and one of the temperance organizers, the Rev. John Coburn, later secretary of the Ontario Temperance Federation, has recorded his opinion that never before had the wet and dry forces been so thoroughly organized as for this battle.[34] The temperance group won, but by only 846 votes.

[32] J. E. Middleton, *The Municipality of Toronto: A History* (Toronto, 1923), I, pp. 327-9.
[33] C. R. W. Biggar, *Sir Oliver Mowat* (Toronto, 1905), II, pp. 527-36.
[34] J. Coburn, *I Kept My Powder Dry* (Toronto, 1950), pp. 68-73.

Provincially, liquor was a dominant issue, with demonstrations, petitions, and plebiscites, promises made and broken, year after year. When war came, it spurred the prohibitionists. A Citizens' Committee of One Hundred was founded at Toronto in 1915, representing all the temperance organizations of Ontario and a number of business men not previously associated with them, and petitions were circulated which gained 825,572 signatures. Toronto was the scene of a major demonstration culminating in the presentation of the petition to the government at the Parliament Buildings. The Ontario Temperance Act, passed in 1916, made the province the fourth to adopt prohibition in a wartime tide which eventually engulfed the whole Dominion, Newfoundland, and Labrador.

In the sabbatarian movement also from the 1840's on, the securing of legislation became primary. In 1845 the legislature of Upper Canada supplemented the Imperial Statutes relating to the Lord's Day which had previously governed the province by a detailed and thoroughgoing act to prevent profanation of the Sabbath. It forbade labour, business, or work (except of charity or necessity); public political meetings; tippling or the permitting of tippling in public places; noisy games, gambling, or racing; and hunting, shooting, fishing, or bathing in exposed situations; it also declared sales and purchases, or contracts and agreements for sale or purchase made on Sunday null and void.

The *Globe* and George Brown led in protesting against breaches of Sunday legislation and advocating stricter laws. Brown for many years presented to the legislature petitions against Sunday labour in the post office and on the canals, and bills which would answer the petitions. A Sabbath Alliance, in which the moving spirit was the Rev. Dr. Burns, then of Kingston, held several demonstrations in Toronto to aid his efforts.[35] The bills were regularly defeated until 1860, when Brown was forestalled by the voluntary abolition of Sunday work in the post office.

The columns of the *Globe* show that the Sunday laws were not dead letters in Toronto and indeed had some public support:

A number of youths, aged from thirteen to sixteen, were enjoying themselves playing "shinty" yesterday on Clare Street. His Worship the Mayor saw their proceedings, and instructed Constable Bradshaw to arrest them. He succeeded in taking a boy . . . and whilst conveying him to the station, an alderman dis-

[35] The Alliance, founded in 1852, also agitated for the closing of saloons on the Lord's Day. This it secured in 1859.

charged him. Justice should not be frustrated in this way. If the law is broken, the offenders should certainly be punished, as a warning to others.[36]

Ald. Sterling asked if the police had received any instructions to prevent young profligates from playing at shinty in the outskirts of the city on the Sabbath day. . . .

Ald. Ewart expressed his sorrow for having ordered the release of a young culprit on Sunday, but he was a very small boy and crying as if his heart would break. The other boys who had been playing were older and had run away.

His Worship stated that it was the duty of the constables to arrest all who were breaking the Sabbath.[37]

Two little boys . . . were arrested yesterday [Sunday], playing at "hurly," on Simcoe Street. They were taken to the Police Station and afterwards dismissed. Twenty-four hours in the cells would be a good means of stopping boys from practices of this kind on the Sabbath.[38]

Yesterday afternoon [Sunday] Constable Archbold arrested four boys for be-having improperly on the streets. They had made a ring on King Street, near Church Street, and while persons were going to worship, they amused themselves spinning tops and playing at marbles. They were taken to No. 1 Station. . . .[39]

In 1885 the Ontario legislature passed an act forbidding Sunday excursions and imposing a penalty of four hundred dollars for its breach. By this time, Toronto's Sunday appears to have been well established,[40] and Major Howland during his two years in office stoutly upheld it. He attempted to give effect to a by-law making it a misdemeanour to hire a horse on Sunday. A case was taken to court but allowed to drop when Howland lost the mayoralty.

In 1888 the Lord's Day Alliance was founded. It grew out of a request from railwaymen to the General Assembly of the Presbyterian Church in Hamilton in 1886, and brought together Presbyterian, Anglican, Methodist, and Baptist representatives. Later, representatives of other Protestant churches and of the Roman Catholic church joined its Board. The Alliance played a leading part from its foundation in almost every case involving Sabbath observance; its vigilant secretaries at the national office in Toronto came to symbolize sabbatarianism there.

A writer described Toronto's Sunday about 1890 as ultra-Scotch.[41] T. Hadley McGinnis complained that in Canada:

[36] Globe, Oct. 12, 1863.
[37] Ibid., Oct. 13, 1863, a report of city council.
[38] Ibid., Nov. 2, 1863.
[39] Ibid., March 28, 1864.
[40] Cf. C. C. Taylor, Toronto "Called Back," from 1886 to 1850 (Toronto, 1886), p. 261.
[41] A. Porteous, A Scamper through Some Cities of America (Glasgow, 1890), p. 84.

Religious rule has made Sunday a terror to the poor, unless one happens to enjoy going to church, walking about the quiet streets, reading, or sleeping. If one is poor, no opportunities for pleasure are had. If one is rich, however, he may drive about in a carriage. . . . Few persons are seen on the street, except in going to or coming from church. On Sunday a Canadian city appears deserted of inhabitants. One may stand on a street corner looking in four directions without seeing a living person or animal.

Most persons disappear for the day, as in a shell, and as completely as if the earth had opened and swallowed them up. How they contrive to do so is a mystery. This is considered, especially in Toronto, "the proper caper."[42]

"Altogether," wrote another visitor, "Sunday in Toronto is as melancholy and suicidal a sort of day as Puritanical principles can make it." [43]

Travellers objected most to the fact that from 1891 to 1897 street cars did not run on Sunday. A clause in its contract prevented the street railway company's operating Sunday cars until the electors had given their approval. The evangelical Protestant churches and the Church of England opposed the cars; the Roman Catholic Church favoured them. On January 4, 1892, there was a 3,836 majority against the cars; in August, 1893, after continued agitation, the majority against them fell to 973. Finally, on May 15, 1897, the vote was 16,372 for Sunday cars and 16,051 against, and public transportation was provided on Sunday.[44]

In 1906, the Ontario legislation affecting the observance of the Lord's Day in Toronto was reinforced by a Dominion statute. It prohibited making sales or doing business or work on Sunday, as did the Ontario Act of 1845, although it allowed certain employees to work if they had twenty-four consecutive hours without labour at another time in the week. It also prohibited holding public games or contests for gain or for prizes, public performances or meetings elsewhere than in a church at which an admission fee was charged directly or indirectly; running pleasure excursions by any mode of conveyance for which a fee was charged; shooting for gain or in such a manner as to cause a public disturbance; and selling foreign newspapers. It forbade advertising any performance or other event which was prohibited by the Act or which, if held in Canada, would be prohibited. This statute, the Lord's Day Act of Canada, has been

[42] *Canadian Notes*, quoted in John Gray's article, "They're Fighting to Save What's Left of Sunday," *Maclean's* magazine (Feb. 15, 1955), p. 32.
[43] W. T. Crossweller, *Our Visit to Toronto, the Niagara Falls, and the United States of America* (privately printed, 1898), pp. 69-70.
[44] In 1897 an act of the Ontario legislature forbade operating of cars by street railways and electric railways for passenger traffic on Sundays.

the whip used by the defenders of Toronto's Sunday for over half a century.

It was during the long period from the late 1840's until the 1930's, in which the moral reform movements were translating their aims into laws, that Toronto established its reputation for respectability. "Anti-Bacchus," writing to the *Globe* in 1848 about the licensing system, asserted that even in Toronto one could find much intoxication on a Saturday evening or Sabbath day.[45] A few years later writers spoke of the city as being distinguished for its morality[46] and as boasting of its respectability.[47] In W. H. Howland's time, Toronto was reputed to be one of the most orderly, law-abiding, and prosperous cities on the American continent, standing "as a practical example of what might be accomplished when honourable, high-handed Christian men are given the reins of government."[48] Its spirit seems to have been well expressed in the combination of piety and profit achieved by the Toronto Coffee House Association, founded in 1881 and dissolved in 1899. This was a band of business men who opened coffee houses, to the number of three by 1890, in order to supply working men with refreshment and social intercourse where strong drink would not tempt them. The coffee houses were financially successful.[49]

In some quarters the city's reputation was not for virtue but for hypocrisy. A traveller of the 1890's wrote:

Toronto is one of the most unpleasantly righteous cities I was ever caught in on a Sunday. Tramways do not run, and the public-houses are closed from seven on Saturday night till Monday morning—not that that makes much difference in Canada, where prohibitionist laws are strict, but not strictly regarded. I had this very amusingly brought home to me. I was being driven about the city by one of the leading editors, who was doing the honours of the place, introducing me to all the leading citizens and institutions. Among other places, we happened on the Toronto Fair or Exhibition, where I was introduced at once to the head, who behaved most mysteriously. He led the way straight into his office cupboard, which fortunately had a ray of light, though it was devoted to brooms and suchlike, till there was hardly room to stand. It was all about a bottle of rye, as they call whisky in Canada, deftly hidden among these Lares and Penates. The exhibition was run on prohibitionist lines weekdays as well as Sundays (though they do not reckon cider alcoholic), and even in the seclusion

---

[45] *Globe*, June 7, 1848.
[46] *Ibid.*, June 7, 1853.
[47] *Ibid.*, July 7, 1854.
[48] A. Scholfield, *Notes on Canada and the United States of America* (Swansea, 1888), p. 21.
[49] D. C. Masters, *The Rise of Toronto, 1850-1890* (Toronto, 1947), p. 184.

of his own office the head dared not offer me a drink until he had hidden me in the broom closet.[50]

The city continued to enjoy a reputation for drunkenness. William Morris described what he saw in Toronto's police court in the 1870's as fearful, and said that such abject-looking wretches as some of the prisoners charged with drunkenness he had never seen before.[51] In the 1890's C. S. Clark wrote that drunkenness was very common, with thousands of arrests made annually and thousands of cases of which the police never heard. The vice, he claimed, was not confined to any one class or one sex. By day drunks were seen reeling through the streets or lying under the trees in the parks; by night there were even more of them. Nor did prohibiting the sale of liquor on Sundays prevent drinking on that day, for many men bought a supply on Saturday night for Sunday use by themselves and their friends.[52]

Still, influential elements in the population subscribed to strict moral standards for themselves, or others, or both. The city was larger[53] and more stratified than it had been, and the groups from which its moral reformers came were less clearly defined. Some of them, however, resembled their predecessors markedly. W. H. Howland, for example, was comparable in social standing to Jesse Ketchum. He was a prominent business man who gave generously to many causes, but he was prevented for a short time from acting as mayor because of financial difficulties.[54] Though he was born in Canada, his father had come from the United States, a fact recalled to his disadvantage while he was a leader of the Canada First Movement.[55] Like Ketchum he was an Anglican, active in the Evangelical Movement.

The rank and file were recruited more widely than before. As well as being drawn from the middle classes they included many working men. In temperance, the shift occurred with the Victoria Reform Society and the rise of the orders. The *Canadian Son of Temperance and Literary Gem*, published from 1851 to 1854 in the interests of the Sons of Temperance, frequently referred to the fact that the

[50] D. Sladen, *On the Cars and Off* (London, 1895), pp. 154-5.
[51] *Letters Sent Home: Out and Home Again by way of Canada and the United States* (Swindon, 1875), pp. 213-14.
[52] *Of Toronto the Good: A Social Study* (Montreal, 1898), pp. 143-4.
[53] From 1861 to 1881 it did not quite double in population, but in the next two twenty-year periods it more than doubled; by 1921 it had over half a million people.
[54] Middleton, *The Municipality of Toronto*, I, 327.
[55] D. C. Masters, *The Rise of Toronto, 1850-1890*, pp. 130-31.

Sons were working men, and castigated the genteel and the respectable as opponents. In one of the last issues the editor, Charles Durand, wrote:

The class in Canada and in this city which does the most to obstruct temperance principles is the genteel class so called. We have just lost two of the number in our midst, both young men, promising, talented, and originally blessed with the strongest constitutions. Will the gentry of this city pause over their fates, untimely and sad, and ask themselves "Should they not now abstain for humanity's sake?" "Is it right for us who are now safe, strong minded, to risk our lives and entice others by our example to meet the wretched end of two of our esteemed citizens in the prime of life?" We ask all intelligent liquor (they may be moderate) drinkers to seriously ponder on these questions. What caused the death of a prominent editor, an ex-chancellor, a county Judge, an eminent lawyer, an excellent young man, all within this year in this city? Is the indulgence of our appetites worth such sacrifices, which are only in fact examples of hundreds of similar cases on record.[56]

The paper also indicated that some of the most vexed problems in the Order, such as transfer from one division to another and the regular payment of dues, were related to the large number of working-class members. Later the *News*, the paper which supported W. H. Howland, combined temperance and labour interests.

As labour grew in strength and organization, it allied itself with the sabbatarian leaders in order to secure a shorter work week. In 1851 a journeyman baker asked the *Globe* for support in a campaign against night work, long hours, and Sabbath desecration. In the 1880's representation from railroaders led to the formation of the Lord's Day Alliance. Labour also supported Howland: Scholfield tells that a deputation of livery-stable keepers waited on the Mayor to ask that they might have the benefit of the rest day, and that the chief of the Knights of Labour in Toronto wrote him expressing gratitude for what he had done towards giving working men a peaceful and quiet Sabbath.[57]

In temperance, the change from open to secret societies and from stress on self-restraint to legal action reduced the support and leadership received from the churches previously most favourable. An item in the *Christian Guardian* for August 20, 1845, indicates the beginning of a rift: "A temperance lecturer says to the public, 'I would suggest the propriety of getting up picnics, processions, and soirees, wherever practicable.' *We* would suggest to the religious public the propriety of doing no such thing." The rift widened as the churches moved from sectarianism to denominationalism and from

[56] Dec. 16, 1854; see also May 13, 1851, and Oct. 11, 1853.
[57] Scholfield, *Notes on Canada and the United States of America*, p. 21.

the morality of the heroic few to that of the respectable majority.[58] Thus the *Canadian Son of Temperance and Literary Gem* in 1852 wished for greater Methodist zeal:

[Methodist] ministers are generally men of talent, and we wish to see this talent, and the zeal they usually display, partly bestowed in furtherance of the principles of our Order. We are aware that many Methodist ministers are with us, but we also know that more stand aloof from, and some oppose our Order. This opposition arises generally from a false view of our principles and their tendency. . . . Among the first to take hold of the [temperance] cause in Canada in 1830, were the Methodist ministers. Those were days of moral suasion. These are days of action and of a better organization, found among the Sons of Temperance. We wish to see Methodism arrayed universally on our side, for our Order.[59]

As the more evangelical churches declined in ardour, the Church of England, especially through the Evangelical Movement within it, and the Roman Catholic Church became more ready to co-operate with the movements of reform. All the religious bodies were interested in protecting rights they shared against what they considered unfair competition. They could thus unite in the Lord's Day Alliance, the Seventh Day Adventists standing virtually alone outside. By the early years of the twentieth century such joint efforts were also possible as the Moral and Social Reform Council of Canada, which brought together the Church of England, the Methodist, Presbyterian, Baptist, and Congregational churches, the Salvation Army, the Evangelical Association of North America, the Canadian Purity-Education Association, the Trades and Labour Congress of Canada, and the Dominion Grange and Farmers' Association.

Politically, temperance and Sunday observance were important issues both municipally and provincially throughout this period. In continuation of the alliance of the Reformers with temperance, the Liberals were considered to favour and the Conservatives to oppose anti-liquor legislation. When either politician or voter had conflicting loyalties, however, the outcome was hard to predict. Hector Charlesworth tells how Sir Oliver Mowat, Premier of Ontario from 1873 to 1896, kept the allegiance of both prohibitionists and liquor interests:

The prohibitionists were mainly to be found in the ranks of what, without offence, I may call the "non-conformist" bodies, and their allegiance to Sir Oliver was based on antipathy to the Anglican Church, which was in the main

[58] R. H. Niebuhr, *The Social Sources of Denominationalism* (Hamden, Conn., 1954), p. 18.
[59] March 3, 1852.

Conservative. . . . The liquor interests, on the other hand, from selfish interest supported the Mowat government, which had the power of life and death over them and did not hesitate to exercise it. The arrangement worked very smoothly, because all Sir Oliver needed to do when the demands of his prohibitionists for action became too aggressive was to send for a few of their leaders and intimate that they must be careful or they would let in the godless Tories.

Hon. G. W. Ross was in a more awkward situation than Sir Oliver. He, like some other prominent politicians, had developed his oratorical powers on temperance platforms, and when he became premier he was besieged by prohibitionist groups:

In the early years of this century, when, because of various political scandals, the feeling was abroad that his government was doomed, men who were not prohibitionists themselves, but zealous for party advantage, urged on Ross that he might save the conscience of the community and make a gesture consistent with his earlier convictions by adopting the policy of prohibition. . . .

"I would not do it if I were a dictator with an assurance of absolute power for the rest of my life," said Ross. . . . "Experience has convinced me that public sentiment in this country is not ripe for prohibition and never will be in my time. Any attempt to enforce such a law would be a failure and would be injurious to the administration of all laws. Especially would it be injurious to the cause of total abstinence which I preached in my youth and have practised all my life."

When prohibition came, it was through a Conservative government:

Strangely enough, it was left to Sir James Whitney to devise the most effective laws by which temperance sentiment could express itself in individual communities, and to his successor, Sir William Hearst, who did permanently banish the bar. Both were Conservatives and despite that fact they went farther in meeting the views of prohibitionists than the professed friends of the movement.[60]

Turning to legal action separated the temperance movement in Canada increasingly from the movement in the United States. The events leading up to the Civil War, the war itself, and its aftermath were also divisive. In Canada, as in the northern United States, temperance people were often strong abolitionists.[61] When the orders were torn by dissension between abolitionist and pro-slavery groups, the setting up of autonomous Canadian organizations was a natural outcome. Further, temperance in Canada did not retrogress as it did in the United States after the war. Such developments as the extension of agitation among women in the Women's Crusade and the

[60] H. W. Charlesworth, *More Candid Chronicles; Further Leaves from the Note Book of a Canadian Journalist* (Toronto, 1928), pp. 190-2.
[61] Women's rights was another cause often combined with temperance. The *Canadian Son of Temperance and Literary Gem* even espoused the movement for reform of female dress initiated by Amelia Bloomer.

Women's Christian Temperance Union continued to affect Canada, however.

In the 1920's, when so many bastions of puritanism were stormed and taken, Toronto appeared impregnable, though government control replaced wartime prohibition in Ontario in 1927. Liquor could be purchased only with individual permits issued annually to adults and subject to cancellation or suspension for abuse, sold only in stores and outlets either operated or licensed by the government's control agency, and consumed only in the purchaser's residence; liquor could not be advertised, and the control agency's decisions could not be appealed.

The prohibitionary laws accorded with the moral standards of important segments of Toronto's population. Middleton compared the attitudes and behaviour of newspapermen in the 1920's and twenty years earlier:

It is difficult for a young man of our time to understand the revolutionary change—of even the past twenty years—in social customs, particularly in the use and abuse of strong waters. The reporter who did not drink was a curiosity. How could he avoid the pressing hospitality of all sorts and conditions of men? How could he reward the kindness of an outsider who was a continual source of news save by the usual invitation immortalized by Mr. Weller, "Sammy, let's mix ourselves a damp"? How could he hope if he were a political writer to be trusted by the major and minor statesmen, if he declined to draw up to the round table of conference and ring the bell in his turn? Suddenly, and long before prohibition was a fact of life, it came about that no one was pressed to drink; fewer and still fewer business men had either the time or the inclination. Politicians and aldermen appeared who had dry proclivities. The newspaper editors "fired" one or two men who missed an assignment by self-induced illumination. Then insensibly, but none the less surely, reporters came to the belief that the only dependable illuminant was midnight oil. Some of the old timers were wedded to the old customs, and the older beverages, but the young fellows were of a new type.[62]

In the 1920's and even the 1930's Sunday continued to be rigorously observed. One visitor found the sabbatarianism inoffensive, since on Sunday morning "the whole world" went bathing.[63] Others formed less favourable views. E. A. Powell wrote:

Sunday in Montreal is devoted to recreation. . . . But Sunday in Toronto is marked by deadly dullness and sanctimonious depression. The streets are deserted. No place of amusement shows a sign of life. Only the churches are open. The last time I was there I came down to breakfast at ten o'clock to find the hotel dining-room closed. I had to walk a mile to find a lunchroom. The people

[62] Middleton, *The Municipality of Toronto*, I, p. 432.
[63] Y. Fitzroy, *A Canadian Panorama* (London, 1929), p. 96.

of Toronto presumably enjoy this rigid observance of the Sabbath, but the city is no place for a stranger on Sunday unless he is piously inclined.[64]

J. H. Stembridge likewise found Montreal gay and Toronto hushed and deserted except for church-goers.[65] Leopold Infeld felt that Toronto was always slow and silent, but especially so on Sunday:

It must be good to die in Toronto. The transition between life and death would be continuous, painless and scarcely noticeable in this silent town. I dreaded the Sundays and prayed to God that if he chose for me to die in Toronto he would let it be on a Saturday afternoon to save me from one more Toronto Sunday.[66]

But puritanism had lost the offensive, and soon began to yield to the forces of change. Soon after prohibition ended in the United States, beverage rooms were opened in Toronto and other parts of Ontario, when in 1934 the law was altered to allow the licensed sale of beer and wine by the glass in hotels, beer parlours, clubs, and military messes. The next year wineries were permitted to set up branch retail stores. During World War II the federal government passed restrictive measures but relaxed the ban on advertising so that distillers and brewers might promote the war effort. The relaxation continued after the war, and Toronto's newspapers, streetcars, and subway displayed institutional advertisements in which the sponsor's names were prominent. The licensed sale of spirits by the glass was allowed in cocktail and dining lounges from 1947 on, after a strongly fought battle between wet and dry forces; two years later the leader of the Conservative government which had brought about the change was defeated in a Toronto riding by a militant temperance crusader and C.C.F. candidate, in part because of the cocktail lounge issue.

The impact of advertising increased in the 1950's with the advent of television, greater use of publishing addresses outside the province by papers and magazines, and the inclusion of product identification in the corporate names of breweries in order to circumvent the prohibition of brand advertising. The Premier of Ontario announced a new code of ethics for liquor advertising on May 31, 1960, to cope with these developments.

The officers of the Canadian and Ontario Temperance federations, the Women's Christian Temperance Union, and some church groups have opposed each successive relaxation of the laws; just after the

---

[64] *Marches of the North* (New York, n.d.), pp. 110-11.
[65] *A Portrait of Canada* (London, 1943), p. 152.
[66] *Quest, the Evolution of a Scientist* (New York, 1941), p. 324.

lounges were opened a mass temperance rally of women was held in Massey Hall; and periodically ministerial conventions have denounced the lounges and the emergence of Yonge Street as "Rum Row." But there has been no sustained large-scale public opposition.

The Dominion Alliance for the Suppression of the Liquor Traffic and its Ontario branch, both with headquarters and secretaries in Toronto, had become quiescent in 1923 under the impact of prohibition and of dissension between extremists and moderates in their ranks. The outstanding extremist withdrew to fight through uncompromising organizations and alone until his death in 1960. The Alliance became the Canadian Temperance Federation, its provincial branch the Ontario Temperance Federation, and revived in the thirties. Both the federal and provincial federations have taken a much less aggressive stand than had the Alliance in former years. Their secretaries have devoted much of their effort to lobbying and education: one of the provincial secretaries mentioned as an outstanding accomplishment the inauguration of a campaign against drinking and driving during the Christmas and New Year period which was later taken over by the police.

Since the thirties, and especially since World War II, temperance activities have been supplemented and even overshadowed by activities centred about alcoholism. Alcoholics Anonymous came to prominence in the Toronto area exactly a century later than the Victoria Temperance Societies which it resembles in many ways. In 1950 the Ontario Government set up an Alcoholism Research Foundation for research, treatment and rehabilitation, and public education; the Foundation has a treatment and educational centre and its head office in Toronto.

Over the years there had been a gradual easing of Sabbath restrictions to permit the opening of the Museum and the Art Gallery, and the sale of foreign newspapers and articles other than drugs. But in the 1940's the rate of change accelerated in Toronto as in other Canadian cities and resort areas. The dissatisfaction of members of the services who spent weekends in Toronto provoked much discussion, but the only action taken was for individuals, churches, and a few voluntary agencies to provide hospitality and non-commercial recreation. Before the war's end, however, an Ontario Justice, reversing a Toronto magistrate's decision, upheld Sunday bowling when the alleys were leased to a non-profit organization, and by 1947 a movement was under way to secure authorization of certain types of commercial sport on Sunday afternoon. In 1948 pre-Confederation Lord's Day legislation was repealed.[67] The sports movement gathered momentum through that year and the next, and reached a stirring climax in the successful campaign to secure a plebiscite, win it on January 1, 1950, and finally secure the necessary changes in provincial legislation.

The Lord's Day Alliance considered the Lord's Day (Ontario) Act of 1950 to be beyond the powers of the provincial legislature. Rather than lay charges against individuals to obtain a ruling, it sought to have the matter settled under the Constitutional Questions Act, but failed. However, in 1958 the Attorney-General of British Columbia asked the courts to decide whether the Provincial Legislative Assembly had the right to alter the charter of the City of Vancouver to permit commercial Sunday sport. The Dominion Board of the Alliance entered the case, and when it lost in the British Columbia Court of Appeal went to the Supreme Court of Canada. There it also lost. Thus the validity of the Ontario legislation seems established.

In the 1950's, in addition to agitation for inclusion of certain activities among the sports permitted on Sunday, there has been increased musical activity on Sunday and the burgeoning of film societies with Sunday meetings. Sunday afternoon concerts, inaugurated in Massey Hall in the winter of 1955 and in city parks in the summer of 1959, went unchallenged because no admission is charged, although some advertising is done and donations are received at the indoor concerts. In 1955 the secretary of the Lord's Day Alliance told the organizers of a series of Sunday evening concerts that charging admission would break the law. The sponsors were university students and the concerts were to be given on the campus. The chamber orchestra involved, the Hart House Orchestra, was young and in a precarious financial position. A storm of protest arose against the Alliance. Eventually it was arranged for the concerts to be given for members of a society who paid dues instead of admission fees. Jazz clubs also began to operate on Sunday in the 1950's. The Provincial government announced in the spring of 1960 that it would bring down legislation to allow non-profit organizations to charge admission fees for "concerts, recitals, and other musical performances of an artistic and cultural nature" on Sunday afternoons, and the Lord's Day Alliance signified its approval. The film societies in the main show movies of limited commercial appeal. They sell memberships cheaply because they rent movie houses and equipment which would otherwise be idle on Sundays: their mem-

[67] There is a possible exception to this: one act is said to have been overlooked.

bers thus have an interest in the maintenance of the Lord's Day Act·

A notable attempt to break down Sunday restraints was the Toronto *Telegram*'s publication of a Sunday paper during part of 1957. The Alliance and the United Church Board of Evangelism and Social Services tried to prevent the innovation, and when they failed the Attorney-General forestalled the Alliance by himself laying charges against the *Telegram* and consenting to charges of working on Sunday being laid by the Telegram against the *Globe and Mail*, the Toronto *Star*, the Canadian Broadcasting Corporation, and the Toronto Broadcasting Company (Station CKEY). The case was delayed for about two years while the C.B.C. argued that as a crown agency it was not liable to charges under the Lord's Day Act of Canada. It lost its appeal in two Ontario courts but won in the Supreme Court of Canada. The Attorney-General of Ontario then refused to proceed against the other defendants for acts which were not offences when performed by the C.B.C. and the charges were withdrawn. The Sunday paper venture, however, had ended long before: it was financially unsuccessful and lasted only seventeen weeks.

While the old moral standards are still adhered to by some sections of the population, they are no longer general among any large or influential groups. The temperance and sabbatarian organizations have dwindled to pressure groups with small professional staffs, volunteer boards, and rather ill-defined constituencies. These are probably still mainly middle-class, but the middle classes are so large and diversified that they also contain many who are indifferent or hostile. Little support now comes from the working class.

In the Sunday sports campaign of 1949[68] both sides wooed the workers. Those advocating change stressed that the Lord's Day Act was class legislation, more restrictive for working men than for the wealthy; those upholding the Act emphasized that it safeguarded the workers' day of rest. Organized labour, at the time facing rising unemployment, revealed neither strong interest nor unanimity. Most union leaders and union locals took no public stand.[69] In the final

---

[68] The Toronto newspapers have been the source of information about this campaign.
[69] Those who opposed the objectives of the campaign included the national director of the United Steel Workers, the second vice-president of the Theatrical Stage Employees and Moving Picture Machine Operators of the United States and Canada, and a business manager of the Carpenters' Union, A.F.L., and a vice-president of the Toronto Building Trades Council. On the other side were a past president of the Ontario Provincial Federation of the Trades and Labour Congress of Canada, and two unions, the Toronto Firefighters' Union and the General Truck Drivers' Union, A.F.L.

days of the campaign, the proponents of Sunday sports accused the Citizens Committee of having employed non-union labour to print its literature. The Citizens Committee countered with a large newspaper advertisement carrying a reproduction of the contract between the printing company that had done its work and the Toronto Pressmen and Assistants' Union, a statement that all composition and printing had been done by fully recognized union members although the union label did not appear through a technicality, and a declaration of opposition to an open Sunday by a union official.

For many workers the right to a weekly day of rest appeared firmly established by 1950. Those whose work-free Sunday is still threatened have been quick to protest against encroachments upon it: motion picture operators, service station attendants, and milk drivers have all done so successfully in recent years. But, for most, attention has passed to the right to enjoy the day of rest as they see fit.

About temperance the major churches have moderated their opinions and activities. They are aware that many in their congregations, including lay officers, are "social drinkers" and are unwilling to alienate them. In the United Church, for example, the secretary of the Board of Evangelism and Social Service sometimes exceeds the temperance organizations in denouncing the "liquor interests"; but a Hamilton minister who in 1957 pleaded for recognition of the fact that many laymen were moderate drinkers and at the same time good Christians received considerable support. Several ministers, including those in upper middle-class districts in Toronto, stated that if they made total abstinence a condition of church membership they would lose large sections of their congregations. The secretaries of the Temperance Federations, clergymen who work and receive funds largely through the churches, consider that their efforts are not always regarded with enthusiasm by ministers. Some churches substitute support of alcoholism research and education for temperance and prohibition activities.

Though the churches vary in attitudes and zeal concerning temperance and prohibition, they keep rank concerning Sunday observance. The Dominion and Provincial Boards of the Lord's Day Alliance now comprise official and unofficial representatives of the Anglican Church of Canada, Baptist Federation of Canada, Churches of Christ (Disciples), Evangelical Baptists, Lutheran Synod of Canada, Presbyterian Church in Canada, Roman Catholic Church, Salvation Army, United Church of Canada, and United

Brethren in Christ; and other religious bodies co-operate. In the Sunday-sports struggle of 1949 in Toronto, the clergy of virtually all faiths ranged themselves on the side of the closed Sunday. A full-page newspaper advertisement, donated by 114 Protestant churches, bore exhortations from the Anglican Bishop of Toronto, the General Secretary of the Baptist Convention of Ontario and Quebec, the Moderators of the Presbyterian Church in Canada and the United Church of Canada, the Commissioner of the Salvation Army, and a representative of non-denominational churches. Toronto's Roman Catholic cardinal and the editor of a Roman Catholic weekly paper, a prominent Jewish rabbi, and the leaders of the British Israelites were among those opposing the relaxing of restrictions. Of the few who did not conform, an Anglican minister attempted to establish a compromise position, a Unitarian minister declared that if the church was worthy it would retain its following in spite of an open Sunday, and the Seventh Day Adventists offered a thousand dollars for biblical proof that Sunday should be kept holy.

So that they might not be accused of standing alone against the tides of change, the religious leaders tried to minimize their role. The anti-Sunday-sports activities were conducted through the Toronto Citizens Committee Opposing Commercial Sunday Sports, which solicited contributions, published leaflets and newspaper and billboard advertisements, and conducted a door-to-door canvass. The name of the Citizens Committee implied breadth of support. Its headquarters staff was described as composed of leading business men, sportsmen, and churchmen. The secretary, a Presbyterian pastor, maintained that the Committee was made up primarily of laymen and that the opposition expressed by the Committee was not simply that of the clergy. Several Committee advertisements listed the names of its lay officers—its honorary chairman, chairman, and treasurer—but omitted that of its secretary.

Arguments for a closed Sunday were stated in humanitarian rather than religious terms. They stressed the right of employees to a weekly day of rest rather than the duty of Christians to keep Sunday holy. The Lord's Day Alliance and church representatives took pains to indicate that, contrary to charges made by the Sunday Afternoon Sports Committee, they were not against "ordinary unorganized sports," but simply against commercial sports. When the leader of the Sunday sports movement called the Lord's Day Act a padlock law against children and against the underprivileged, the secretary of the Lord's Day Alliance pointed out that economy rather than law dictated the locking of sandboxes and swings in parks and play-grounds on Sunday, and that non-commercial recreation such as fishing, swimming, and golfing was no longer illegal; he went so far as to advocate giving young people a chance to play and enjoy them-selves.

That the majority of electors voted for commercial sports on Sun-day was interpreted as indicating a decrease in church influence. The *Canadian Forum* pointed out that since Toronto municipal voters are largely a middle-class, tax-paying group, it was extremely unlikely that all or even the great majority of "yes" voters were outside the Christian churches, and concluded that:

People are increasingly unable to believe in the disinterestedness of the churches, or in their ability to distinguish a moral issue from one that merely appears to threaten their social and economic position. That the churches are spending far too much of their energies in an inglorious rearguard action against the inciden-tal vices of society; that they cannot distinguish cause from effect in social evil; that they have not only tended to retreat into the propertied middle class, but are no longer coming to grips with the real needs of even that class....[70]

Except for such instances as the Sunday sports plebiscite, moral issues have ceased to be vital political issues. Elections, either munic-ipal or federal, are now rarely fought about liquor, although in the summer of 1960 the newspapers attempted to make it play a part in the forthcoming mayoralty contest. Provincially, although the Con-servatives are still considered less and the Liberals more favourable to temperance and prohibition, and although the Co-operative Commonwealth Federation has within it a small knot of prohibi-tionists, liquor is handled in gingerly fashion by all parties. Nor are Sunday laws something upon which politicians normally take a stand. During the campaign preceding the 1950 plebiscite, when it was nec-essary for candidates for municipal offices to declare themselves, thirty-five pronounced against the city's seeking legislation to make commercial sport legal on Sunday, six were in favour of it, ten were undecided or unwilling to state their position, and one could not be reached for comment by the newspaper which took the poll. The positions taken suggest that the candidates were predominantly middle-class and that they assessed public opinion as opposed to Sunday sports. The newspapers seem to have made the same assess-ment: all opposed Sunday sports, one from the first and two after some hesitation. Once a majority had voted in favour of the sports, however, the newspapers altered their position. In the incident in-

[70] February, 1950. See also the Toronto *Star* editorial of Jan. 3, 1950.

volving the Hart House Orchestra all three censured the Lord's Day Alliance, although one later voiced some second thoughts.

Toronto has served for a hundred and thirty years as headquarters for temperance and sabbatarian organizations and activities, fulfilling a role normal to cities as centres of communication. Throughout the period much of the support of the movements has been rural: indeed, feeling has been directed against Toronto and other cities as hotbeds of vice, strongholds of Satan, where the Sabbath is desecrated and the hydra-headed monster intemperance revels.[71] Nonetheless, the rallies held in Toronto and the policy statements issued from Toronto have helped to mould the city's reputation.

The support of moral reform in the city, however, has not depended simply upon its serving as a centre of moral reform movements. The city has for a substantial part of its lifetime had a puritanical ethos which has made it not only an appropriate host to moral reform demonstrations and offices but also a crucial element in the strength of the movements. Its citizens in considerable numbers have enrolled in temperance societies and orders; it has passed and sometimes enforced "blue laws"; it has impressed travellers with its strait-laced attitudes and behaviour. There have always been groups in Toronto's population which were neither pious nor sober. The fulminations against the lax in the literature of the moral reform movements, the newspaper accounts of court cases, and the descriptions of those who wished to convict the city of hypocrisy all testify that in Toronto as in England the Victorian Age "contended with tumultuous underground pleasure,"[72] or at least with the activities for which pleasure is a common euphemism. But although abstemiousness and strictness have been practised assiduously by only a minority, the minority's attitudes have until recently dominated the customs and laws of the community. They do so no longer.

The sharp decline in Toronto's puritanism is frequently attributed to its changing ethnic composition. The economic opportunities opened up by its entrepreneurs have drawn a steady flow of immigrants. Some have come from rural and small-town Canada and presumably have reinforced its temperance and sabbatarian norms. Others have come from abroad: the proportion of the city's population born in continental Europe rose from 5.15 per cent in 1911 to

[71] The words are those of an editorial in the *Journal of the American Temperance Union* for August, 1838.
[72] V. S. Pritchett, "The English Puritan," review article in the *New Statesman and Nation* (Jan. 26, 1951), p. 103.

8.25 per cent in 1941 and to 12.72 per cent in 1951 and is still rising. It is often assumed that the Europeans have different drinking customs and Sunday observances from old Torontonians or others whose cultural background is Anglo-Saxon, and that their attempts to perpetuate their ways affect Toronto attitudes and patterns of behaviour. The French, Italian, and Slavic names of tavern keepers and the predominance of non-English-speaking people at Sunday afternoon concerts are cited in evidence. Before the 1950 Sunday sports plebiscite the secretary of the Citizens Committee commented that because Toronto was distinctly British it would not follow the example of Windsor, with its cosmopolitan population, in voting for an open Sunday. After Toronto had done just that, another clergyman coupled the foreign-born with Communists as being responsible for the results in Wards Four and Five, the only two of six wards favouring Sunday sports where the majority was large.[73]

The importance of immigration is easy to exaggerate, however. In the nineteenth century, both in the United States and Canada, newcomers quickly shed moral traits differentiating them from the rest of the population. Their theologies were alien, but the necessities of daily life, including the need for the good opinion of their neighbours, engendered puritanism in them.[74] In the mid-twentieth century, if new arrivals have retained their own standards, it has been because of decreased pressure upon them from the society into which they have moved. A recent newspaper survey claims that statistical analysis reveals little correlation between the number of immigrants in Ontario and the amount of liquor consumed.[75] When changes in law have been related to altered attitudes and customs, the influence of immigrants is further diminished by the time and property restrictions of the franchise. When the Sunday sports plebiscite was held, many recent arrivals were not well enough established to meet municipal voting requirements.

It is tempting to explain the decline of puritanism by the worldly success of its practitioners. In the early years, temperance and sabbatarianism were promoted by the middle classes who were seeking changes not only in men's moral standards and behaviour but in the social, religious, economic, and political structures of the day. By the mid-century they had achieved many of their objectives, and in

[73] Three wards opposed Sunday sports, only one by a large majority. The three—Wards Seven, Eight, and Nine—were all away from the centre of the city to the east, west, and north.
[74] M. L. Hansen, *The Immigrant in American History* (Cambridge, Mass.,1948), chap. V.
[75] *Globe and Mail*, Nov. 23, 1959.

doing so become part of the *élite* of the society. The process mellowed them; they and their families began to live graciously, though they may have continued to advocate sterner ways for others. The economic institutions which they had developed could, as Weber has pointed out, continue; and if as they joined the upper classes, from whom moral reform has never received strong support, their places in the middle ranks had been replenished by other ascetic Protestants, the moral standards of the community could have remained unshaken also.

How long replenishing continued is hard to determine. From about 1840 down to World War I there was some correspondence between the aims of the moral reformers and those of an increasingly self-aware and organized working class. This brought to temperance and sabbatarianism the breadth of support necessary to secure their political objectives, but it was essentially fortuitous and it concealed a slackening of zeal in the middle classes. Since World War I and even more since World War II, there has been no alliance with labour and withdrawal of middle-class support has become increasingly apparent.

As Toronto has grown to metropolitan status, its middle classes have ceased to uphold themselves and to impose upon others with fervour and unanimity the norms of temperance and sabbatarianism. A few people, chiefly in the lower middle classes, cling to the old standards. Many more, particularly in the ranks of business executives, salesmen, and professionals, are less imbued with puritanism than their predecessors and do not consider drinking behaviour and Sunday observance as grave moral issues. Some regard teetotalism and rigid sabbatarianism as intolerance and bigotry, to them forms of immorality more reprehensible than lack of self-discipline. Toronto's changing ethos and reputation are largely due, then, to one of the most striking phenomena of modern urban society, widely recognized and much moralized about by such men as C. Wright Mills, David Riesman, and William H. Whyte, Jr., but not yet sufficiently analysed: the new middle classes.

The Place of the Professions
in the Urban Community

O. HALL

THE GROWTH AND SPREAD of the professions is a salient feature of modern urban life. Urban living centres in work, in specialized occupations. Professions are specialized occupations, but specialized in a distinctive way. They provide services that in the normal pattern of events are used only on highly infrequent occasions by the majority of their clients. (Perhaps only once in a whole lifetime does a client require a surgeon to remove an appendix, a minister to marry him, or a lawyer to draw up a will.) Professionals, so conceived, could survive only among aggregates of population large enough to provide a statistical assurance that their services will be required frequently enough to assure them a livelihood. The more specialized the service that the professional has to offer, the larger must be the community in which he can subsist.

The purpose of this paper is to explore, if not to answer fully, three questions. How have growth and change in the urban community affected the ways in which the old-established professions carry out their respective bundles of tasks? What, for these professions, are the consequences of the emergence of the more recently professionalized occupations? What are the results of these developments for other parts of the social order? The initial reference is to the Toronto community; most of the discussion is generalized, however, and not restricted to a specific local area.

Historically the most respected professions have been medicine, law, and the priesthood. (The army, also with long-established claims, is excluded for the purposes of this discussion of urban life.) Over recent decades these have been supplemented by others: by a range of newer professions, by some premature professions, by some pseudo-professions, and by some lowly occupations eager to lift themselves so as to share in the prestige that the professions enjoy. This expansion of the professions in the urban environment is a complicated affair, involving three main currents of growth. There has been an expansion of the older professions and a consequent splintering into more specialized forms; new professions have arisen through the provision of services based on previously unused knowledge; and there has been a great deal of activity among occupations aroused by an admiration of the ancient professions and attempting to model themselves upon them with greater or lesser success.

If one proceeds to study this growth with reference to census data, it is clear that the growth has been an uneven affair. For the city of Toronto as a whole the professions, *in toto*, as listed in the census, have been growing faster than has the total working force of the community. Between the years 1931 and 1951, the total working force in the metropolitan area grew by approximately 80 per cent; for the professions listed the growth has been approximately 95 per cent. However, this growth has not been evenly distributed among the older and newer types of professions. The census includes nursing and school teaching (which have been largely the preserve of women) among the professions and shows these to have grown over the two decades at approximately the same rate as has the total working force. The same pattern of growth appears for the classical masculine professions, law and medicine. (For the priesthood, there has been negligible growth, much less than for the working force at large.) Hence among both men and women there is a pattern of modest growth for the older professions, roughly the same as the growth for the working force in general.

On the other hand, there is a much more pronounced rate of growth for the professions on the newer fringes. Thus for men in the category of "draughtsmen and designers" the numbers have increased from approximately 800 to 2,800 in the two decades, an increase of 250 per cent; for women, the category of "authors, editors and journalists" has climbed from 120 to 360, an increase of 200 per cent. For both men and women the modest average changes in all professions conceal much larger changes in a few professions.

The growth of the professions can be viewed profitably from another direction. Reference was made above to distinctly masculine and distinctly feminine professions. Whatever has been the historical pattern, there is a noticeable tendency for masculine roles to be invaded by women; at present there is almost no profession that can literally be called a masculine prerogative. In 1931 there were no women listed among the clergy; by 1951 there were eleven. Indeed, in some cases it seems that the women are tending to drive the men out of specific professions. During the two decades under discussion the number of women librarians has doubled, whereas the number of men in the field has declined absolutely.

On the other hand, there is a comparable tendency for men to move into fields traditionally feminine. In the field of social work, the women workers have approximately doubled in the period in question, but men, during the same period, have more than tripled in number. The same phenomenon can be observed in school teaching. Here the number of women has increased 40 per cent in the twenty years, whereas the number of men has increased 100 per cent. These shifts in the composition of a profession indicate that the two sexes are in competition in such fields; but whether they are competing for the same kinds of jobs, or whether the field is casting up two distinctive kinds of jobs (one filled by men and the other by women), is a matter for study.

From the above discussion it should be clear that the professions represent a very lively part of the occupational world. Among them several kinds of competitive struggles are occurring simultaneously. There is a struggle going on at the borders between professions; within specific professions, there are struggles between different kinds of people striving to gain a foothold therein or to maintain a foothold there. New professions are challenging old ones, some of which, indeed, may be shuffling off the scene.

This lively character of the professions poses numerous serious problems for the various kinds of people who try to record the numerical changes occurring among occupations. Within relatively short periods of time completely new species may arise. It is not surprising, therefore, that the occupations which the census lists under the heading of "professions" should differ somewhat from those which a sociologist would so classify. The census excludes some occupations which come close to the fringe of being professional in nature and includes some of doubtful credentials. It includes doctors and nurses in the health field; it also makes a place for chiropractors and osteopaths, even though the latter two practitioners may be considered non-professional by the doctors and nurses. On the other hand, it does not include undertakers, whose trade begins precisely at the point where that of the doctor ends; and similarly it excludes pharmacists who not only are recognized by doctors as having an important role in the healing process, but are taught (as are undertakers) in universities, and on occasion by doctors themselves. Along with priests and clergymen, representing the most ancient of professions, the census finds a place for nuns and lay brothers, yet neither group necessarily is engaged in work that can be called professional. Similarly, on the fringe of law, one finds that judges and magistrates are included; however, even though these may at one time in their careers have been lawyers, they belong, for the moment, in the category of dignitaries who preside over special institutions rather than in the class of people who render some sort of professional service.

The Nature of Professions

In the light of the variety of occupations included in census classifications of professions, and of the comparable occupations that are excluded, it is desirable to state the essential characteristics of professions. From the standpoint of the sociologist's interest in work, the essential matters are not those of the specific duties performed, or of the attributes of those performing the work, but rather the social exchange that goes on and the social relationships that emerge from the exchange.

The great historic professions of civil life have been medicine, the priesthood, and the law, as we have said; from these we may construct a model which will be useful in considering their position and that of other professions later on the scene. Each has been concerned with a distinctive need of the human animal. The physician was the person who could restore some measure of ease to the diseased; the priest could provide salvation for the troubled soul; and the lawyer could find a solution for the entanglements in which people found themselves. Disregarding for the moment the differences between these, and the idiosyncracies each displays, there exist some obvious similarities. Each supplies some specialized service that canot be supplied by the needy person himself or by the jack-of-all-trades. The service is supplied directly, not through an intermediary or an administrative staff. In each case the recipient of the service is in some sort of danger—bodily, mental, or physical. In each case he must trust the practitioner to be his *alter ego*, that is, to act for him with the care and sense of responsibility he would exhibit if he himself were the needy one. Because illness and kindred troubles strike at unscheduled times, the practitioner must be constantly available; he must in large degree be at the beck and call of the client. Moreover, in order to permit the practitioner to deal with the matter effectively, the client must not only follow the directives of the professional but must refrain from complicating matters by making use of other practitioners during the course of the relationship.

The nature of the exchange that goes on between the professional and the client makes it possible for the former to demand a high return for his services. (Here we are speaking mainly of medicine or the law.) If one is in danger of losing one's life or one's worldly possessions, the person who can help one avoid such catastrophes could conceivably ask for most of the second category and find the client ready to part therewith. The blend of a highly significant service and of a substantial reward for the provision thereof accounts in large part for the prestige of the historic professions. It gives to them a peculiar luminosity as compared with the general run of occupations in society. At the root of all the great professions there lies this constellation: a specialized service, often of a hazardous nature; a client in danger; and a set of arrangements that permit the former to come to the aid of the latter.

The profession so conceived can be profitably distinguished from the *organized* profession. This comes into existence when the practitioners of a profession become self-conscious about their work, develop collective concern for their destiny, and take collective steps to fit their work and themselves into the social order. It does not follow, as a matter of course, that the organized professions will take steps that are beneficial to the profession either in the short or in the long run. Indeed, the members may adopt policies that are detrimental in a high degree to the survival of the profession in question. They may make an unwise selection of their successors, by recruiting the wrong kind, or too few, or too many; they may train them in an ineffective fashion, perhaps according to a set of unworkable dogmas; they may organize themselves in a fashion that precipitates conflict and hostility with other parts of society; they may demand rewards of such a nature (either excessively high or low) that they prejudice their very survival. The organized profession may deal realistically with the problems of the profession *per se* or be singularly inept.

The general features of an organized profession can be briefly listed. They comprise machinery to recruit newcomers to the profession, machinery to train these recruits, machinery to control competition within the profession, devices to deal with competing groups outside the profession, and mechanisms to deal with the larger public.

The specific social devices that arise in the organization of a profession are the most readily visible features of a given profession, and may become its most significant attributes. By way of illustration, if a profession trains its new members in a university setting this attribute is clearly understandable by those without. Similarly, if its members utilize distinctive office procedures, use a calendar for appointments, require payment in the form of a fee, establish a public code of ethics, organize an association that holds meetings, and so forth, these attributes become the highly visible aspects of the profession in question. In general, the attributes are the most readily recognized features of a profession, while the nature of the profession as such is likely to be concealed by the very things that people take for granted about such a type of work.

These three aspects—the historic model, the organized profession, and the attributes of the profession—provide useful distinctions for the social scientist who is interested in professions and their place in society. They are not the usual distinctions made in general commonsense discussion of professions. Moreover, the generally high prestige that professions have enjoyed has been the product of all these items seen as an undifferentiated mass. On the other hand, whenever other occupations have attempted to model themselves on the admired professions, they have usually selected for imitation one or another of the attributes of the profession, even though this item may turn out to be far removed from the essential core. There is currently a perverse sort of illogicality in many occupations whose members seem convinced that if they can copy a few of the attributes of historic professions they will thereby come to share the essential nature of such and consequently share in the prestige of their admired models.

Professionals and their Troubles

So far this paper has argued two points: the occupations warranting the label "professional" are not exact counterparts of the ones conventionally so classified in censuses; the field of the professions is a lively, shifting affair, whose boundaries are in considerable flux and whose centre is far from stable. We shall now go on to consider the current status of established professions and the consequences of some of the developments in more recent professions.

These two topics are closely interrelated. It is the highly visible prestige accorded to the established professions that makes them so attractive to many occupations in our society which are, by contrast, relatively formless and in many cases somewhat unsatisfying to the practitioners thereof. On the other hand, there is an anomaly here. Precisely at the time when a large number of occupations are attempting to ape the model of the established professions, the latter find themselves in deep trouble. Many of them find themselves diverging far from their historic model, while others find it progressively difficult to approach that model.

By way of illustration, census data indicate that the old independent professions are giving up fee practice and are turning to salaried practice. The census for 1951 indicates that of the 1,632 physicians and surgeons in the Toronto area more than one-third are listed as "wage earners." Among notaries and lawyers the proportion working for salary or wages is somewhat higher. This means that in these old historic professions a considerable proportion are not adhering to the ancient model of an independent practice by which, for a fee, they provide services for clients; rather they are providing services for a single powerful client, or for an outright employer. The model of their work lives has become less that of a profession and more that of a modern bureaucracy. (Some observers claim that the same process can be traced out with respect to the priesthood, which likewise has become enmeshed in its own bureaucratic machinery.) It is especially noteworthy that, in the case of the medical profession, this development has occurred contrary to the express wishes of the members, and in large part in spite of their active opposition.

Among Toronto architects even fewer can make a livelihood as independent practitioners dealing directly with a body of clients. Thus among them, in 1951, over 70 per cent were classified as salaried workers. It is clear that, as one of the newer crop of professionals, they are far removed from the model of independent practice. Their troubles, however, have another root. Only a small proportion of the people who build houses sense a need for the services of an architect. Builders can manage without their services entirely, or may substitute the services of a draughtsman for those of an architect. Moreover, there is not much that architects can do to establish a durable demand for their services. Hence they are seriously limited in their efforts to develop a clientele to support them financially. Architects to date have achieved very little of the success of doctors and lawyers in establishing a wide and unchallenged demand for their distinctive services.

If the architect has extraordinary difficulty in creating a demand for his services, the pharmacist has suffered from the opposite condition. Although his self-image is that of a fellow-worker of the doctor, giving specialized attention to compounding medicine for the doctor too busy to do so, fate has decided against that image. He has many people demanding his services, but these people require him to be the salesman of a great variety of non-medical goods, rather than a clever compounder of esoteric drugs. They view him as merely another retail merchant or salesman. Moreover, they tend to act towards him as customers rather than as clients. What is more, the genuinely professional component in his services is continually being whittled away by the transfer of the main job of compounding remedies from the pharmacist's shop to the large pharmaceutical house. As a result, the part played in the drama of medical care by the pharmacist seems slated for a progressive decline. The road to survival requires him to become more retail merchant and less professional man. It would seem, however, that success as a retail merchant fails to compensate for the loss of prestige involved in this loss of a professional function.

When one turns attention to the position of the engineer in present-day society the model of a professional man serving a set of clients is almost totally inapplicable. Of the electrical engineers (who are the most dependent of all engineers on salaried employment in the city), the proportion in independent practice is approximately 1 per cent. The remaining 99 per cent are strictly employees. This state of affairs has become abundantly apparent to many of the members of this occupational group. They realize not only that they are salaried workers, who are hired in large numbers by a few powerful employers, but also that collective bargaining is their appropriate relationship to their employers. However, this realization does not necessarily diminish their desire for professional status and for the prestige accorded to professional work.

For the engineer, as for the architect, the claim to professional status hinges largely on the fact the training goes on within the university setting. As noted above, this is one of the obvious attributes of the doctor and of the lawyer, whose training schools have been traditionally associated with great universities. However, the mere fact of being trained in a university setting can do little to modify the basic character of the work of an occupation. Moreover, in many cases the climate of university training may be more apparent than real. The bond between the engineering student and the university seems very tenuous when compared with that of medical and law students. There is very little of a pre-professional or extra-professional component in their training. Few engineering students follow through on their professional training by turning to graduate studies or specializing in the intellectual components of their training. The very fact that engineers in many parts of the world are trained in technical institutes rather than in universities emphasizes the incidental nature of the bond between engineering student and the university *per se*. This realization is a matter of concern to many engineers who have developed an anxiety about their professional status, and the basis on which they may legitimately continue to claim to be professionals.

Nurses, on this continent, seem to be acutely sensitive to the problems of status in their profession. One evidence of this is the degree to which, over the past decade, they have launched studies aimed at exploring the sources of their discontent with their lot. These studies are aimed mainly at discovering the various kinds of subspecializations that have sprung up in the nursing field, and the relation of these to the larger world of work.

The claim of the nurse to professional status is a peculiar one. To begin with, the nurse does not make her livelihood by serving her own set of clients as an independent practitioner. Of the 1399 women in the nursing profession in Toronto listed by the 1951 census, every last one indicated that she worked for salary or wages. Moreover, with rare exceptions, nurses are trained, not in the university setting, but in the places in which they work. Their daily work involves them in taking orders directly from the supervisors in the hospital, or in slightly less direct way from the doctors on the staffs of the hospitals. Hence, in terms of both income and work organization, nurses lack the relative independence from an employer usually associated with professional status.

On the other hand, the nurse is closely associated with the drama of dangerous illness. As in the case of the undertaker and the pharmacist, some of the aura of prestige surrounding the doctor is cast over her. In the situations which she works in a hospital setting she has a peculiar relationship to the doctor. Although she is an employee of the hospital, she is also the right-hand man of the doctor, and therefore on occasion is entrusted with responsibilities far greater than those with which she is formally entrusted. This informal arrangement permits her to share in modest fashion in the prestige allotted to the doctor.

Nursing seems to have acquired a number of distinctive anomalies. The nurse is poorly paid, but her professional orientation prevents her from engaging in collective bargaining. She has employee

status, but because of her distinctive relationship to the doctor she
acts at times on the basis of her own responsible judgment. She is
recruited often from the lowly ranks of society, and occupies a lowly
position in the hospital hierarchy, but she associates with the figures
of topmost power and prestige in the hospital setting. Each of these
adds a peculiar dimension to her claim to professional status, and
each is the source of status anxieties on her part.

The largest category of professionals, as listed in the census, is that
of teachers, who comprise over 20 per cent of the total. As noted
earlier, in this field of work the men are the invaders and seem to be
displacing women to some degree. This tends to divide the field in a
significant way, as is seen in the fact that the teachers' organizations
tend to split into a men's and a women's model. On top of this the
teaching body splinters along religious lines to some degree. These
divisions along sex and religion tend to blur the unity of the whole
group. Indeed, within the field of teaching many members express
doubts as to whether there can ever be an organized profession.
They note such things as the rapid turnover in positions of many
teachers, the use of teaching as a door to the marriage market on the
part of many women, the subordination of teachers to government
officials at the municipal and higher levels, the highly varied levels
of training undergone by the members. These things are seen as
obstacles to the emergence of an organized and relatively autonomous profession,

In their efforts to achieve professional status, school teachers face
difficulties which are much more fundamental than the above discussion suggests. To begin with, teachers are caught in a dual bureaucracy. The model of the autonomous teacher in charge of a one-
room school is becoming an anachronism. Nor is this independent
model any longer a major ideal. The major goal of teachers is to find
a place in the large and increasingly bureaucratized schools in the
urban areas. Work in such situations approximates to that of other
large bureaucracies where the objectives of efficiency, economy, and
uniformity set the tone of the daily activities of the teacher. Rules,
regulations, and ritualized procedures take precedence over the
interests and wishes of teacher and student.

In this context the machinery of bureaucracy grows with little
encouragement. Administration becomes a large element in the daily
work. Some teachers find that they are almost totally immersed in
administrative tasks to the exclusion of teaching *per se*. The emergence of such a bureaucratic structure is apparently one inducement

to men to enter what has been largely a feminine field; they see themselves as progressively emancipated from the teaching tasks, wearing the administrator's garments rather than those of the teacher.

The bureaucracy of the school system *per se* is paralleled by the larger bureaucracy of government within which the school itself operates. Whether or not the school itself is highly bureaucratized it is almost always part of a long and firmly established bureaucracy of the province which has organized the system of schools. Although this bureaucracy seems to be remote from the local scene on which the teacher carries on his work, still it decides in large measure what shall be the content of the teacher's work; it may also carry on an inspection concerned with the quality of the work performed. The very remoteness of this second bureaucracy may add to the sense of the teacher that the control of his work is vested in centres far beyond his own competence and initiative.

The existence of this larger bureaucracy has always been something of a threat to the emergence of a teaching profession of a self-controlling sort. The matter of what services the teacher provides, and, indeed, the matter of access to the field of work, have been vested in an outside body. Thus there have been serious limitations on the emergence of a definitely organized profession for teachers. As indicated above, the newer bureaucracy of the local system poses other threats, whose character can as yet not be clearly formulated. Indeed, from both directions, teachers seem to be becoming progressively enmeshed in bureaucratic machinery rather than moving towards the model of an independent profession.

Yet another feature of the position of the teacher remains to be noted. The relation of the teacher to the client is a peculiar one. Clients do not come to the teacher as autonomous persons in need of help. In most cases they are sent to school by parents, and the exchange which goes on involves both the student and one or both parents. This triadic relationship complicates the professional relationship of teacher and student in manifold ways. The parent may attempt to usurp the position of teacher; he may ally himself with the teacher against the student; he may ally himself firmly with the student against the teacher; or the two parents may split into separate camps and further complicate the professional role of the teacher. In general, one can say that the existence of any third party in the relationship poses very real difficulties for any practitioner of a profession. For the teacher this danger is endemic.

Furthermore, the third party may intervene at strategic points in the system other than that of the teacher-student relationship. The parent may intervene in the local system; he may go directly to the principal and thereby add another complication to the relation of teacher to the bureaucratic system of which he is a part. At another level, the parent as voter has power to intervene in the larger political system which governs the school; this also lies in the background as another complication in the roles played by the teacher. It is scarcely possible for the teacher to remain unaware of the varied ways in which parents act as a third party in the interchange that goes on between teacher and student (or client); the threats to the professional role are equally apparent.

In tracing a few of the troubles faced by the occupants of these various roles some common threads appear. In each case an effort is being made to maintain or achieve a professional model for its organization. A professional model is a blueprint of the hopes of an occupational group. One major element in the model is the client relationship, a delicate blend of the numbers of clients and their power relative to the practitioner. Presumably an ideal clientele for a true profession can be specified. It would comprise enough clients to provide a good living, but not enough to rob the professional man of control over his own time. Some should come from a social class permitting him to act as benefactor, some from a social level sufficiently high to add lustre to the practitioner serving them. Some should possess social power which can be used to further the interests of the profession; none should be strong enough to make the professional man subordinate to them. This list could be extended; it is sufficient to indicate some of the built-in hazards of professional life.

For some activities the number of clients is clearly inadequate to support their hopes to be recognized as full professions. In others clients are as powerful as the head of a giant bureaucracy, capable of transforming the would-be professional into a salaried employee. With others again, the potential client acts as only a customer in a market place should act. For still others the client and the practitioner are related through a third party who is able to modify the tone and character of the client-practitioner relationship. In all of these the achievement of the blueprint model collides with some of the stubborn facts of the social order in which it is set. However, even where the encircling social system hinders the anticipated emergence of the model, that system may be modified in crucial ways by the efforts of the occupation striving for professional status. By way of conclusion, some comments are in order regarding this development—the impact of professionalization on the vulnerable elements in the social order.

One Man's Solutions are Another Man's Problems

A comparable consideration of other professionalized occupations would no doubt indicate ways in which their aspirations for a place in the social order have come into conflict with the obstinate facts of the structure of society. One would like to inquire, about the professions discussed above and others as well, how they respond to their discoveries about the facts of social organization. In some cases, they appear oblivious to such facts; in other cases, they misinterpret them seriously; in still others, they attempt an orderly study of such facts, occasionally by making use of social scientists or by training themselves for that task. From another point of view they respond to their respective situations by engaging in political action; that is, they locate enemies in the social order as well as neutrals and friends. They launch attacks on some, attempt coalitions with others, and strive to elicit the support of still others. In some of these encounters they fail; in some of their advances they are rebuffed; in some areas they encounter suspicions where they had expected support.

An exploration of the politics of the old-established and the newer professions, either in terms of their relative success or of the techniques of political struggle utilized, is beyond the scope of this paper. It will terminate with a discussion of one professional problem and the common solution devised for it.

Most of the professions or near professions considered above are engaged in a debate on how best to train their new recruits. This is accompanied with a concern for the manner of selecting the recruits in the first place. Each of these activities represents an enduring and recurring concern for a profession. However, the amount of attention focussed on these matters and the intensity of the debate suggest that perhaps these matters are also symbolic of more fundamental and less tangible difficulties faced by the professions.

Whether or not this is the case, the character of the solutions is noteworthy. In both cases there is a tendency to solve the problems by handing them over, almost in their totality, to outsiders to solve. The outside agency selected is the university. The consequences of this manner of solving the problems are just starting to emerge. Although one might anticipate that professions, brought into contact with other professions and other parts of the university, would harmonize in some sort of unity, this is not necessarily the case. It would appear that the establishment of professional schools on the campuses of universities is no guarantee that the members thereof will come to understand each other's problems or develop favourable attitudes towards each other. Indeed, proximity may serve mainly to reinforce hostilities and suspicions that have arisen in earlier circumstances. For example, close contact between schools of commerce and professional economists does not necessarily lead to mutual love. The relations between the faculty of a school of dentistry and that of a medical school do not necessarily mellow as time goes on; nor do those of medical schools and schools of hospital administration improve. Incidentally, all three of these lie in the same general area of human life, and are non-competitive in their work. Closeness, like familiarity, may indeed breed contempt.

In those cases where there is an element of competition in the relations between professions, the closeness of common membership in campus life may serve to accentuate and dramatize this element of competition and transform it into conflict. Thus an institute of clinical psychology may find that its relations with a department of psychiatry become progressively chilly, even though both are dedicated to help alleviate a common set of human problems. Similarly, on the borders of pastoral theology and psychiatry, on those of medicine and osteopathy, on those of law and accounting (those concerned with taxation), the similarity of goals does not lessen the conflict engendered by competition. This conflict tends to be all the more severe in so far as one profession considers itself to have prior proprietary rights to a specific kind of work and views the newcomer, not as a helper in a common task but as a downright trespasser. The newcomer, fired with some degree of idealism and of missionary zeal, comes readily to view the established competitor as a block to progress and as a monopolist mainly concerned with protecting its vested interests.

Although there are serious discouragements facing newer professions on university campuses, and despite the disillusionments they suffer, new candidates for professional status arise apace. Long before they appear at the front door of the university to ask admittance to the company of professional schools, they are likely to troop around to the side doors swelling the demand for extension courses. In the beginning they may conceive their needs modestly, perhaps requiring only a single course, such as Real Estate Marketing, to supplement the armament of practical knowledge their members have amassed from work experience. Later this arrangement may be expanded to form a sequence of courses. Eventually these may be systematized, and a certificate issued to the students which differentiates the "trained" members of the occupational group from the rank and file. Later these course requirements may be increased to require a year of residence during which the worker must forego some part of his income. On the conclusion of this more extended training he may receive a diploma rather than a certificate. Such developments on the part of an occupational group bring it near the point where it can claim that it is necessary for all the early training of its members to be carried out in the university setting. It may assert the desirability of a university degree to distinguish the legitimate practitioners from the quacks and charlatans not so trained. By this time, the feasibility of a licensing system will probably have been explored. A new "profession" will have arisen. By such means are the vexing problems of training workers and selecting recruits for training solved in our society.

By this time the wheel may have gone full circle. Of those who came to the university campus as a place to plead for training, some may not only have come to occupy teaching posts there but may also take the position that they, and they only, are competent to train the practitioners in their own discipline. In such manner do universities on this continent grow and develop.

The centralization of training in the university setting, and the consequent separation from the practical world of such matters as training and selection, may gradually isolate the professional school and the organized profession in mutual fashion. The teachers may see their function as that of continuously challenging the accepted procedures in professional life, whether these be technical matters or matters of the social relations and obligations of the profession and the public. The leaders of the organized profession, on the other hand, may continue to view the function of the school as a device for training in the currently accepted procedure, and/or as a gifted spokesman to protect the interests of the organized profession whenever these are endangered or challenged.

The situations discussed in earlier parts of this paper, those in which potential competitors are arising and new procedures are emerging, tend to accentuate the gap between the teaching part of a profession and the practitioners thereof. In such circumstances the critical assessment of current professional practices, or attempts to introduce ideal solutions, are likely to run counter to the demand for practical training aimed precisely at strengthening the competitive position of the practitioners in their respective positions. Thus organized architects are likely, when faced by competition from draughtsmen, to see much of the programme of schools of architecture as mere frills, and to criticize it accordingly. Similarly lawyers, as they see their historic tasks taken over by laymen of various sorts, may push for more practical kinds of training and denigrate many of the interests of lay teachers. Nurses' associations, as they see some nursing tasks taken over by lay workers and other tasks transformed by changes of technology over which they have no control, may look askance at current enthusiasms of nursing teachers and at the solutions to professional problems offered by those teachers. Medical associations, faced by political problems too complex for them to handle effectively, may detect traces of treachery in the staffs of medical schools who fail to support them whole-heartedly. Dentists, fending off the competition of denturists, may view their professional schools as poor defenders in their time of need. Pharmacists, faced by competition by other kinds of merchants and rendered partially unnecessary by the very growth of the industry of which they are a part, may view their professional schools as unrealistic in the face of the problems they face from day to day.

In each of the above cases the source of the gap between the professional school and the corresponding professional body is somewhat distinctive. In each case, however, the results have common features. A split develops between the teachers and the practitioners. Among the former something of a garrison mentality emerges. The teaching contingent polarizes into those who take a professional point of view and those who take an idealistic point of view regarding their present and future. In so far as these things occur, life among the professional faculties of a university has a different pattern than that of the non-professional faculties.

For the university as a whole these matters take on another significance. As indicated above, the nascent professions gradually come to comprise an increasing segment of university life. Usually there is little administrative opposition to such patterns of growth. The addition of certificate courses, of diploma courses, and of new degree courses may be viewed as commendable evidence of growth for the university, and of service to the community into the bargain. As in the addition of a new child to a fertile but improvident family, "one more" does not appear to change things very much. In the course of a decade or two, however, the situation may change to the point where the newcomers outnumber the established members. Conceivably the newcomers may strengthen their host institution by introducing new kinds of people and new kinds of knowledge. However, if, as suggested earlier, the problems which the new professions turn over to the universities are symbolic of more serious problems for which so far no solutions have been devised, the universities may face added difficulties in the days ahead. Professional troubles may become university troubles. Meanwhile, for better or for worse, the rise of new professions will have left permanent imprints on the character of universities.

Social Control and Professional Self-Government: A Study in the Legal Profession in Canada

P. J. GIFFEN

WHEN CONFRONTED with the extensive powers of self-government granted to certain professions in Canada, it is logical for the sociologist to ask questions about the nature and degree of control by the larger society over the use made of these powers. Although formally "free," the governing bodies of the professions do not operate in a social vacuum. If a profession is found on examination to have used its powers in a manner compatible with the "public interest" as defined in the dominant value system, we are justified in looking for the means of social control that have helped to bring about this state of affairs. We can postulate that adoption of policies in the public interest is most likely to result when the situation in which the organized profession must act is such that meeting or anticipating higher levels of public expectations become conditions for safeguarding or attaining important interests of the profession. Although truistic as a general statement, the proposition focusses our attention on the way in which various sanctions serve to bring into relationship the interests of the profession and the expectations of the public, and leads us to make more explicit the content of these three categories. Our case study will be certain changes that have taken place in the organized bar in the common law provinces of Canada since the late 1920's.[1]

In order to practise, a lawyer must be a member in good standing of his provincial governing body, called the Law Society in all the common law provinces except New Brunswick and Nova Scotia, where the term Barristers' Society is used. The executives of the governing bodies, called the Benchers in some provinces and the

---

[1] This article is based on material gathered on a grant from the Survey of the Legal Profession in Canada.

Council in others, are elected for terms ranging from one year to five years, and usually include some ex-officio members. (For convenience we will use "law society" and "benchers" as the generic terms for all provinces.) The law societies have been delegated by provincial statutes control over admission to the profession, power to investigate the conduct of members and suspend or disbar them, the right to collect admission fees and annual fees, and sundry other powers. The professional statutes also define the unauthorized practice of law and prescribe penalties, with degrees of stringency varying between provinces.

Because the law societies have as members all the practising lawyers in their jurisdictions, they have been the logical instruments for collective action at the provincial level. Hence, they have tended to perform many of the functions associated with voluntary professional organizations, as well as being licensing and disciplining bodies; they make representations in behalf of the profession, hold annual meetings (except in Ontario), and study and implement a great variety of measures. The organization of the profession is complicated because a large number of voluntary organizations also exist and perform some of these functions at various levels, although their views are most frequently translated into action through representations to the law societies. In a general analysis concerned with fairly common patterns, we can treat the organized bar as if it were a relatively homogeneous body; the division of labour between organizations, differences in the characters of provincial bars, and the processes leading to the resolution of differences of opinion within the profession must be left to discussion elsewhere.

We shall deal with two of the many changes of policy in the organized bar during the period under review: the adoption of reimbursement funds and the organization of free legal aid. Both are new measures that would clearly be defined as socially beneficial according to prevailing values. The reimbursement fund is a means whereby the law society assumes the responsibility for repaying in whole or in part the financial losses suffered by the clients of defaulting solicitors (although the law society may reserve the right to refuse claims). The capital in the fund is secured by an annual levy on the lawyers of the province. Legal aid plans are the equivalent of public clinics in the medical field; through organization these schemes rationalize the provision of legal services to individuals who are unable to pay fees. The development of public relations programmes on the part of the bar will also be mentioned because such programmes are a response to many of the same circumstances that led to the other two measures, although they are not incontestably in the public interest.

The establishment of reimbursement funds by law societies is a recognition that defalcations cannot be prevented entirely by the methods of control over admission, the accounting rules, or the disciplinary measures that have yet been tried. In the 1930's several of the law societies altered their procedures to expedite the handling of discipline cases and six of them passed rules regarding trust accounts, making it mandatory for solicitors to keep trust funds and personal funds in separate bank accounts. A law journal of that period commented: "Strict discipline, essential as it is, is not sufficient, and no discipline however strict can prevent defaults occurring with the resulting loss to a client and a black eye to the whole profession. Something more is required if the conviction is to be instilled in the minds of the public that under no circumstances will they lose through a defaulting solicitor."[2]

The "something more" that came to prevail was the reimbursement fund. A modified form of "the New Zealand Scheme" was first recommended to the profession at a national gathering in 1931,[3] and the first fund was set up in Alberta eight years later. In the next two decades funds were started in six other common law provinces: Manitoba (1943), British Columbia (1949), Saskatchewan (1950), Ontario (1953), New Brunswick (1954), and Nova Scotia (1957).[4]

The history of organized free legal aid can be traced from 1929, when the Canadian Bar Association passed a resolution recommending locally administered legal aid for the bar, as a result of five years of considering the problem. In 1932, the Law Society of Alberta set up committees in each judicial district to provide legal aid in litigation only, and in 1939 the Law Society of Saskatchewan followed the same plan. During this period panels of lawyers were organized in several cities in various provinces by local bar associations, working in conjunction with social welfare agencies, to provide free legal advice as well as counsel in litigation. The first legal aid clinic meeting at stated periods to interview applicants was started by the Law Society of Manitoba in 1938. However, the greatest growth in organized legal aid clinics has taken place since the World War II. The

[2] Editorial *Saskatchewan Bar Review*, III (1958), 65.
[3] *Programs and Handbook: Fifth Conference of the Governing Bodies of the Legal Profession in Canada* (1931), p. 52.
[4] The Nova Scotia Barristers' Society created a token fund in 1950 but discontinued it in 1952, without having paid any claims.

beginning of this period was marked by a 1947 resolution of the Canadian Bar Association recommending strongly that legal aid schemes be set up across Canada by the profession, a resolution sent to each of the governing bodies. The most comprehensive of the schemes was started by the Law Society of Upper Canada in 1951, providing for legal aid clinics throughout the province under county directors.

A "public education campaign" by the profession was proposed in a national gathering in 1928, but no action was taken.[5] The first venture into institutional advertising was in 1932, when the Law Society of Saskatchewan ran four narrative advertisements in a farm weekly, emphasizing the advantages of consulting a lawyer. The first continuous newspaper advertising scheme was sponsored by the Manitoba Bar Association from 1944 until 1951, when a change was made to radio advertising. The law societies in Saskatchewan and British Columbia both began advertising schemes in 1947; Saskatchewan abandoned the experiment in 1950 after creating a reimbursement fund, and British Columbia changed to radio advertising in 1953. The Law Society of Upper Canada began the most ambitious of the newspaper advertising schemes in 1952 but has since discontinued it. Newspaper and radio advertising, expensive measures having intangible results, appear to have been passing phases, but more subtle techniques of gaining favourable publicity have been used with increasing frequency[6] and at least one law society employs the services of a public relations consultant.

How have the forces of social control served to bring about these changes? Let us first delineate in general terms the types of sanction to which the profession is subject from outside. Two interrelated sources of sanctions may be distinguished: first, laymen as individuals ("the general public"); second, legislatures and governments.

Members of the public wield sanctions as clients or potential clients, and as the people who give or withhold the expressions of evaluative judgment that can be summarized as prestige. Laymen directly influence the livelihood of the profession, within the limits of general economic conditions, through myriad decisions about consulting lawyers. They may secure the services they need from "encroaching" occupations, or consult nobody if they fear that

[5] "Report of the Committee on Encroachments on the Lawyers' Sphere of Activities," *Proceedings of the Canadian Bar Association*, XIII (1928), 371.
[6] These include public forums on legal questions, the provision of speakers for "lay" organizations, publicity releases, and collaboration in the preparation of radio and television programmes of a dramatic nature.

lawyers' charges will be too high, that expensive and troublesome complications might result, or that their money cannot safely be entrusted to lawyers. Or they may abstain simply because they do not know that legal advice is advantageous in certain transactions. Thus prevailing stereotyped ideas about the profession and conceptions of the need for legal advice help to determine the total income of the profession.

The importance to members of the profession of laymen's expressions of approval or disapproval is difficult to isolate, but the frequency with which lawyers have expressed concern (even in periods of relative prosperity) about the negative attitudes of the public toward their profession shows a fairly high level of sensibility. The comments of lawyers indicate a strong sense of injustice, a feeling that widespread misconceptions have cheated them of the appreciation to which they are legitimately entitled: "A fairly general failure to understand the value of the service he performs renders complete recognition of his place in the scheme of things impossible. In fact, it may be said that there is no class of men so misunderstood and unappreciated."[7]

The work and status of lawyers are affected in so many ways by legislation and by the administrative policies of governments that it would be impossible to do justice to the subject in a short paper. We shall confine our discussion to the sanctions that have been of most frequent concern at the provincial level. The power of the provincial legislature to pass enactments governing professional groups means that disfavour may be expressed by rescinding some of the profession's powers of self-government or reversing decisions of the law societies. The possibility has been kept before the profession by events in several provinces since 1925. A number of these threats to the profession deserve mention.

When the Law Society of Upper Canada raised the educational standards for enrolment as a student-at-law in 1926, the move was interpreted in the Ontario legislature as an attempt to limit numbers by discriminating against poor boys, and the following year the legislature passed an amendment to the effect that all changes in the rules and by-laws made by the Benchers had to be approved by the Lieutenant-Governor-in-Council. The restriction was later withdrawn but the lesson was frequently recalled within the profession. In 1941, one of the leaders of the profession in Ontario stated: "If the governing body were free to pick and choose at their will who

[7] J. W. Wilton, "Why the Law," *Manitoba Bar News*, V (1932), 1.

should be admitted as candidates to the Bar, the situation would be simplified to a very great degree, but to attempt to do that would obviously incur the displeasure of legislative bodies, and quite properly so, and the control would quickly pass out of our jurisdiction."[8]

In the 1930's the Ontario legislature on three occasions exhibited its power by passing, over the opposition of the Benchers, special bills making lawyers of individuals who could not meet the Law Society requirements. A legal journal, in commenting on the hearing on one of these bills, indicates that the enactments provided occasions for the expression of hostility toward the profession: "Enquiries directed to the representative of the Benchers, as to, for instance, how many of the profession were in gaol, and other remarks of that nature, are only straws in the wind indicating the temper of the legislature as a whole towards the profession as a whole."[9]

Events in several other legislatures have also shown how easily sentiment in favour of curtailing professional privileges can be mobilized. In Saskatchewan an amendment was passed in 1936 providing for an appeal to the Court of Appeal from a refusal of the Benchers to readmit a disbarred lawyer, although the Law Society opposed it. Three years later in Prince Edward Island the legislature passed an amendment making possible an appeal to a Judge of the Supreme Court from a refusal of the Law Society to admit an applicant to the bar. The premier, a lawyer, opposed the amendment, but was deserted by his cabinet colleagues and could muster only two supporting votes after a debate that brought forth strong criticism of the legal profession.[10]

During the 1930's proposals to make the bonding of lawyers compulsory were discussed on a number of occasions in several legislatures. Compulsory bonding has usually been regarded by the profession as a threat to its autonomy on the grounds that bonding companies would be given power to say who could not practise law. When, during the 1938 session of the Alberta legislature, it became apparent that legislation for compulsory bonding was imminent, the Law Society was able to avert this humiliation by promising to start a reimbursement fund. A similar series of events led to the creation of a reimbursement fund in Manitoba in 1943. The fact that the threat of action by Parliament played a considerable role in the

[8] *Minutes of the Fourteenth Conference of the Governing Bodies of the Legal Profession in Canada* (mimeographed, 1941).
[9] Editorial, *Fortnightly Law Journal*, VII (1938), 273.
[10] *Charlottetown Guardian*, April 13, 1939.

creation of the Solicitors' Compensation Fund in England in 1941 was well publicized among leaders of the profession in Canada.

More recently, the investigations into the powers of the several professional societies in Saskatchewan in 1946-8 and in Alberta in 1950-1, have been a reminder that professional autonomy is retained at the pleasure of legislatures. In neither case was the legal profession singled out for special attention, the expressed concern being the powers of all the professional monopolies to exclude applicants for admission.[11] The result in Saskatchewan was parallel amendments to nineteen professional acts. In the case of the legal profession the amended legislation provided that all by-laws as passed had to be laid before the legislature which had the power to nullify them, that the Attorney-General could initiate new hearings for disbarred or suspended members, and that examination of all candidates for admission was to be placed under the control of the University of Saskatchewan. The effect of these changes was to make it much simpler for the legislature and the government to intervene in the affairs of the profession at any future time. The only change brought about in Alberta was to place the examination for admission entirely in the hands of the University of Alberta—not a drastic measure in view of the close collaboration between law faculties and the organized profession that prevails in most provinces.

The favour or disfavour of legislatures can also be expressed through a variety of legislation affecting "encroachments" on the services that the profession would like to reserve to itself. Of special importance to the profession are statutory definitions of unauthorized practice and the penalties attached, the statutory privileges given to competing occupations, and the power of, and rights of appearance before, administrative tribunals. Throughout the profession, the desire for more stringent statutory protection has been expressed on innumerable occasions over three decades. However, the law societies more frequently than not have refrained from having bills for amendments presented because they felt that the temper of the legislatures was unfavourable, as illustrated by the following quotations:

One of our greatest practical stumbling blocks was the fact that our own Act was woefully deficient in its delineation of what we considered to be (for want of a better term) our rights. Year after year we approached the Government attempting to get something done but year after year we were dissuaded for fear

[11] The shortage of medical doctors for rural communities appears to have stimulated the inquiry.

of the opening up of the Act affording an opportunity of members deleteriously affecting even what we had.[12]

It is the considered opinion of this committee that the remedy lies through propaganda or, perhaps it might be better stated, through education of the public rather than through legislation. To conserve to the members of the Society the practice of law and particularly conveyancing would perhaps interfere to a considerable extent with the earnings of persons practising conveyancing. This must be taken into consideration, along with the sometimes unfavourable atmosphere apparent when the legislature is approached with regard to amendments to the Legal Professions Act.

Furthermore, your committee believes that unfavourable public opinion might be aroused if stringent amendments were sought.[13]

When an attempt was made to introduce a bill to enable the profession to forestall some of the more flagrant encroachments on its sphere, the mover of the bill had to leave the house to escape the storm that broke over his devoted head.[14]

The Society and Council have been endeavouring for several years to remove from the Barristers Society Act a provision permitting Justices of the Peace to draw or prepare any instrument relating to real estate. The strong opposition in the Legislature, particularly from members residing in rural areas, has defeated our efforts.[15]

Behind the use of sanctions by the public and legislatures lie expectations regarding the behaviour of professional organizations. The law societies, like the individual practitioner, are expected to exhibit concern for the public welfare in their behaviour, to forego the exploitative possibilities of their advantageous position where the interests of clients and the larger society are affected. The granting of powers of self-government appears to imply an agreement that the powers will be used to maximize the standard and availability of the professional service. When self-interested behaviour is suspected, the apparent breach of trust seems to arouse strong indignation, and terms such as "labour union," "closed shop," and "monopoly" in reference to the profession are common. The fairly pervasive distrust of professional privileges manifested in some of the events related above seems to create a more or less continuous burden of proof on the self-governing profession.

[12]Unpublished report of the Treasurer of a Law Society, 1939. Access to unpublished reports and minutes of organizations was granted to the writer on condition that the sources would not be identified.

[13] "Report of the Commitee on Encroachments", Law Society Gazette (Saskatchewan), II (1939), 9.

[14] Editorial, Fortnightly Law Journal, II (1942), 194.

[15] Handbook: Twenty-First Conference of the Governing Bodies of the Legal Profession in Canada (1949), p. 28.

If the public's expectations of professional societies remained constant, an equilibrium might eventually be achieved, but the long-run tendency has been for the level of expectations to rise as the values associated with the welfare state have gained wider accept-ance, thus creating a continuous incentive to change. With the in-creasing responsibility of the state for welfare has come the increas-ing acceptance of state control over interest groups as a legitimate means. For some professions the trend has brought new demands and an implied threat. Where the services are regarded as important to individuals regardless of status, one demand has been that the services should be made universally available by some means. The medical profession has obviously been under much stronger pressure than the legal profession because of the importance attached in our society to medical care. Although there has been no significant public agitation for subsidized legal aid in Canada, the trend of the times has been sufficient to create in the minds of some lawyers apprehension about "socialized law." The possibility was occasionally used as an argument within the profession in the 1930's and 1940's, and later the events that led to the appointment of the Ruschliffe Committee by the British Government toward the end of World War II were interpreted as the handwriting on the wall. In arguing for a legal aid scheme at an annual meeting of one of the law societies, a proponent stated (erroneously) that "in England it has been taken out of the hands of the profession and a system approaching socialized law has been adopted."[16] Even if legislative action to bring about legal aid is only a remote possibility, the trend of public opinion is such that a profession that allows the needy to go unserved is liable to criticism, while the one that does not is likely to be applauded.

The protection of clients from defaulting solicitors is also sub-sumed under the prevailing welfare values. Being a victim of a de-faulting solicitor is a form of undeserved individual misfortune, one of the host of contingencies bringing suffering that ought to be alle-viated in a welfare system. The bonding of various other occupations handling trust funds had either become mandatory or was generally practised in order to win public confidence by the time that public demand for the compulsory bonding of lawyers was voiced in the 1930's. The publicity given to defalcations by lawyers served to bring the changing values to bear in a specific demand, and the events in Alberta and Manitoba showed that the threat of legislative compul-sion was real. Proponents of the measure in other provinces argued

[16] Unpublished minutes of a law society, 1950.

that greater credit would accrue to the profession by anticipating legislative pressure and acting voluntarily. An additional argument, based on the experience in New Zealand and in Manitoba, was that more stringent legislation against encroachments might be secured as a reward for creating a reimbursement fund.

If the profession does not act in this matter the public will through legislation. The latter happening or even delay in bringing about the former will result in further harm being done to the regard in which the profession is held by the public. On the other hand only the most favourable and widespread publicity would result from the taking of such a step by lawyers themselves and nothing would do more to raise the profession in the estimate of the public.[17]

It is manifest that bonding is an accepted safeguard for trust monies, and it is my sincere submission that becoming discernment counsels anticipatory and voluntary action on our part. Then, over and above all the considerations detailed, we grow in the public esteem and break down some of the mistrust with which we are regarded.[18]

We have always pointed out that not the least of the advantages of the voluntary adoption of the New Zealand Scheme would be that it could be used as a bargaining means to obtain a real measure of protection for the profession from the trespasses of the unqualified practitioner. The Manitoba Statute seems to prove our point. Sooner or later all the legislatures of the common law provinces are going to take the view that if the profession is to retain its privileges, it must in some way safeguard the public from defaulters.[19]

Some of the main interests of the profession have emerged in the previous discussion and need not be reiterated. Lawyers, of course, share with other occupations the desire to improve their income and prestige, and they share with other self-governing professions the belief, justified or not, that any loss of autonomy to laymen will have highly undesirable consequences. An examination of the effect of changing circumstances on the urgency of specific interests during and following the depression will help us to understand the concern of the profession with public opinion and legislative favour.

The sharp decline in lawyers' incomes with the depression focussed the attention of the profession on "overcrowding" and "encroachments," both matters of concern in earlier years but now much more pressing.[20] "It is well known," wrote a lawyer in 1929, "that in the

[17] "Resolution of the Sault Ste. Marie Law Association," *Fortnightly Law Journal*, XII (1942-3), 40.
[18] "Address of C. C. McLaurin (J)," *Saskatchewan Bar Review*, IX (1944), 48.
[19] Editorial, *Fortnightly Law Journal*, XII (1942-3), 306.
[20] Between January 1919 and December 1920, forty resolutions relating to "unqualified practitioners" were passed by the Ontario Bar Association.

legal profession generally, only a limited number have large and lucrative practices, a large number make only a fair income and are forced to spend with economy, while a considerable number cannot at law alone make even a bare living."[21] And a western Canadian lawyer stated in 1936: "Saskatchewan has over five hundred lawyers. There is small doubt one hundred could do all the work offering quite well."[22]

Although some lawyers advocated arbitrary limits on admissions,[23] leaders of the profession were sensible of the opposition that any attempt to restrict entrance, even by raising educational standards, might arouse in legislatures. Consequently, efforts were directed to exploring all avenues that might lead to more business for lawyers. The number of radical measures that were discussed, although never seriously pressed, shows the ferment of the period. The following item, one among a list of suggestions contained in a report of 1929 that received national circulation, is an example:

MEET COMPETITION: Make it professional for solicitors to conduct any class of business in any way akin to legal matters, such as insurance, real estate, sales and loans, collecting rents and interest, auditing accounts, acting as agent or attorney, managing estates and property, etc. For this purpose to seek modification of the code of legal ethics and thereby to permit lawyers to advertise the lines in which they specialise. . . .[24]

"Encroachments," a long-run problem of the profession, became a matter of special concern since a limit on numbers was not feasible. The nature and variety of the services lawyers perform had made the profession particularly susceptible to competition. With the aid of standard forms and a knowledge of the few immediately relevant procedures, laymen in bordering occupations could perform such tasks as conveyancing, drawing wills, preparing mortgages, and even incorporations.[25] Furthermore, several new specialized agencies and occupations—prominent among them trust companies, collection

[21] B. J. Maclennan, K.C., "Encroachments on the Lawyers' Sphere of Activities", *Proceedings of the Canadian Bar Association*, XIV (1929), 264.
[22] Western Canadian subscriber, "Encroachments", *Fortnightly Law Journal*, V (1936), 250.
[23] In 1938, a county law association in Ontario sent a resolution to the Benchers "deploring the failure of the Law Society of Upper Canada to effectively deal with the problem of restricting the number of practising lawyers," *Proceedings of Convocation*, Jan. 19, 1939, p. xii.
[24] R. J. Maclennan, K.C., "Encroachments on the Lawyers' Sphere of Activities," *Proceedings of the Canadian Bar Association*, XIV (1929), 267.
[25] Most of the provincial acts dealing with the legal profession appear to have been originally based on the English Law Society Act of 1843, in which the only forms of "unauthorized practice" anticipated were court work and advising on the law.

agencies, and chartered accountants—had either cut into the lawyers' traditional field or were playing a large role in developing fields, as the accountants have in taxation matters. The growth of administrative tribunals was helping to decrease litigation, especially in the Prairie Provinces. Commenting on the effect of experience before tribunals on the attitude of laymen to lawyers, a Saskatchewan lawyer said in 1938:

They have also learned that they can do just about as well by themselves before the boards and tribunals as they can with legal assistance. Notaries public and justices of the peace are also appearing before the boards and tribunals, both federal and provincial, and making representations on behalf of clients with just as much success (or lack of it) as a lawyer would have.[26]

The occupations and agencies believed to be offering competition to lawyers were numerous indeed.

A list of those who encroach on the lawyers' field of activities, as gathered by the questionnaire, is as follows: Notaries public, Commissioners for taking affidavits, Justices of the Peace, trust companies and their various officers and clerks, loan companies, insurance companies, insurance agents, insurance adjustors, motor accident adjustors, real estate agents, auctioneers, branch-bank managers, chartered accountants, collection agencies, postmasters, law stationers, druggists who sell will forms prepared in Scotland, medical doctors, retired teachers, clerks of small debts courts, liquidators and trustees in bankruptcy, other company executives, credit associations and the laymen who secure offices requiring legal knowledge such as police magistrates, land registrars, court registrars and sheriffs.[27]

A startling convergence is found in the numerous discussions of means of dealing with encroachers and of tapping the reservoir of demand among people who consulted nobody about legal problems. Whatever specific remedies were proposed, the problem tended to be formulated ultimately as one of improving the public's opinion of the profession. More stringent statutory protection against unauthorized practice, itself dependent on public favour, was seen by some as being of limited usefulness.

Senator Farris pointed out that the profession have at last realized that their services cannot be forced upon an unsympathetic public and that unless the lawyer as a class can convince the public that his services are valuable and desirable, no amount of coercion or special privilege will produce a demand for these services.[28]

---

[26] *Saskatchewan Bar Review*, III (1938), 88.
[27] "Memorandum on Encroachments on Lawyers' Acitivities", *Proceedings of the Canadian Bar Association*, XVI (1931), 223.
[28] Editorial, *Saskatchewan Bar Review*, III (1938), 37.

The public will seek out anyone who can do the work better or cheaper, and all the amendments in the world to the Legal Professions Act will not solve our difficulties. . . . We must satisfy the layman—our very existence depends on our so doing—that we can do the work better, that his interests are better protected and better served in our hands.[29]

Many considerations appear to have contributed to the emphasis on "educating the public" as a means of offsetting encroachments. Not only was the securing of sufficient evidence to prosecute difficult, but such prosecutions often brought negative reactions among local people. Moreover, many of the developing specialties that competed with lawyers—such as trust companies and chartered accountants—were sufficiently established that statutory proscription was out of the question. In some provinces, discussions with trust companies led to informal agreements defining a division of labour[30] and some changes were made in law school curricula to better prepare lawyers for developing fields, but members of the lay public were still regarded as the ultimate arbiters. No amount of prosecution of competitors or informal agreements with them, it was argued, would significantly increase the demand for lawyers' services; this called for a change in prevailing attitudes to the profession.

That "institutional advertising' should have been proposed and discussed with increasing frequency after 1929 is perhaps the best indication of the importance the profession attached to changing popular stereotypes. Whether "institutional" or not, advertising is a form of activity associated with business, and advocates of the measure had to overcome considerable opposition from lawyers who felt that even "dignified" collective advertising was contrary to traditional ethics. Many felt that:

the Law Society, but not individual members, should adopt a policy of polite and indirect but persistent systematic advertising as a means of correcting many misconceptions about the profession and its principal competitors, as a means of fostering a more friendly relation between lawyers and the public, and to inform the public that no expenditure bears larger returns than that made for legal advice.[31]

---

[29] G. L. Fraser, "Encroachments," Paper delivered at the Annual Meeting of the Law Society of British Columbia, 1939 (pamphlet), p. 3.

[30] Following a resolution of the 1931 Conference of Governing Bodies: "That each Governing Body be requested to appoint a special committee to confer with the managers of Trust Companies and to make representations as to the unfairness of their methods in seeking to take legal business from the lawyers." Several law societies engaged in such negotiations, as well as conferring with associations of real estate agents, insurance agents, and chartered accountants.

[31] Law Society Gazette (Saskatchewan), March 1934, p. 5.

Your Committee... is of the opinion... that any scheme which might be adopted would sooner or later have the appearance of advertising intended to bring business to lawyers and would not be in keeping with the traditions of the profession.[32]

We must protect the younger members of the Bar and must meet the competition of Trust Companies and Real Estate Agents.... We must combat dignified advertisements of Trust Companies by like advertisements.[33]

The preoccupation with public relations is also seen in the arguments put forward by the proponents of reimbursement funds and, later, of legal aid schemes. The conception of the reimbursement fund as a means of bringing generalized approval to the profession as well as combatting the specific competition of trust companies had gained currency before the adoption of the fund in Alberta in 1939 made legislative compulsion a pressing consideration. After that date, reports of the favourable effect on the public of the Alberta Scheme added weight to the public relations argument. In 1943, a Bencher of the Law Society of Alberta wrote:

The fund now has the strong support of the great majority of the members of the Society. They would be strongly in favour of its continuance even if all legislative pressures were removed. The prestige of the profession and the confidence of the public in it has undoubtedly been greatly enhanced and this has rebounded particularly to the benefit of the young practitioners.[34]

The public relations value of organized free legal aid does not seem to have been a consideration in the early years but we can see the beginnings of an appreciation in a 1934 report of a local legal aid clinic:

Several unemployed and labor organizations have passed resolutions expressing their appreciation and at least two newspapers... have contained editorials of congratulations. From comments heard, the service appears to be creating a more friendly attitude in the public mind towards the profession than has hitherto existed in Saskatoon.[35]

This may be compared with more recent statements:

Public Relations Committee; Mr. A. J. Cowan, Chairman, reported that his committee had met again. It felt that the question of legal aid was very important in respect of public relations. He suggested the appointment of a special committee to go into the whole matter of legal aid for the Province.[36]

[32] Law Society of Upper Canada, Proceedings of Convocation, Jan. 15, 1948, p. xxiv.
[33] Minutes of a bar association, 1940.
[34]S. W. Field, "The Assurance Fund of the Law Society of Alberta," Canadian Bar Review, XXI (1943), 592.
[35] Law Society Gazette (Saskatchewan), March 1934, p. 5.
[36] The Advocate, VII (1949), 56.

The Society does not advertise the skill of the profession. However, the organization of Legal Aid in this Province has resulted in excellent publicity or advertisement.[37]

There is no doubt that legal aid, in Ontario certainly has been one of the best public relations movements that the profession has yet discovered.[38]

The preoccupation of the profession with public opinion is not due solely to circumstances peculiar to the period since the late 1920's. Unfavourable stereotypes of lawyers have a long history, and the sensibility of lawyers is probably of equally long standing. This endemic unpopularity of lawyers[39] is of some importance in explaining the vulnerability of the profession to negative sanctions in the period under review.

The high valuation attached to collectivity-orientation[40] in our society is reflected in the animus directed at individuals who are expected to be disinterested but are believed to fall short. Certain aspects of the lawyer's role seem to lend themselves to an unfavourable interpretation of his motives. The public is prone to see members of the profession as helping "guilty" criminals to gain acquittals, advising wealthy or corporate clients on how to "get around the law," profiting from encouraging prolonged litigation, and creating and maintaining complex procedures for effecting apparently simple transactions. Moreover, the public is well aware that lawyers participate in various capacities in business and politics. Since these are spheres in which self-orientation is expected to prevail, lawyers tend to become tinged with guilt by association.

When the legal and medical professions are compared, we can see that it is much more difficult for lawyers to communicate the rationale behind their procedures and, in general, to project the image of selfless dedication that doctors, with the assistance of the mass media, have managed to enjoy. Doctors appear to be always on our side, since illness is universally accepted as undesirable. And they move in a cloistered world of the healing arts that shields them from mundane associations. This is not to say that doctor's motives are never questioned, but rather that they have been much less prone to unfavourable stereotyping than lawyers.

[37] Annual report of a law society, 1952.
[38] Editorial, *Chitty's Law Journal*, IV (1954), 3.
[39] The sources of this unpopularity are discussed at greater length in P. J. Giffen, "The Legal Profession and the Public," *Obiter Dicta, New Series*, I, 23-6.
[40] Talcott Parsons, "The Professions and Social Structure," *Essays in Sociological Theory* (Glencoe, Ill., 1954), pp. 34-49.

The aggressive component in the prejudice against lawyers, however, appears to be disproportionate to the amount of unacceptable behaviour attributed to them. Perhaps some of the psychological processes involved in ethnic prejudice operate to the disadvantage of lawyers, particularly the displacement of aggression. Once lawyers have been identified as legitimate targets through unfavourable stereotyping, they may fall heirs to aggression displaced from other frustrating objects. The frequency of expressions of anti-lawyer sentiment in the legislature of the Prairie Provinces in the 1930's seems to support the thesis, in that it indicates a tendency for the hostility to increase with widespread economic deprivation.

Such public sentiments are an important factor in the readiness of a supposedly conservative profession to consider, and eventually adopt, new measures. Not only does the prejudice against lawyers help to engender genuine threats to the profession in critical periods, but it also creates a large element of uncertainty, since the swings in public opinion appear to the profession to be highly capricious. New policies that go beyond the minimum public demands serve to diminish the risk. If the legal profession is found to have been more adaptable than the medical profession in attempting to create a fund of goodwill, part of the explanation may lie in the experiences and skills that go with the lawyer's role. One would expect that the participation of lawyers in negotiation, compromise, and manipulation in spheres of complex interaction would result in less of the collective obduracy that appears to characterize some of the policies of the medical profession.

The tendency of the organized bar to change in recent years has also been affected by a process that might be called cumulative legitimation. As more jurisdictions in Canada and other common law countries have adopted a particular policy (or raised certain standards), the burden of proof has shifted from the advocates to the opponents in the jurisdictions that have not done so. And, in addition to enhancing the moral responsibility, experience elsewhere has helped to establish the feasibility and efficacy of new measures. Through legal periodicals and direct inquiries, developments in other Commonwealth countries have been made known to the profession in Canada and, within Canada, there has been a high degree of communication between provinces, especially through national meetings and legal journals. The reimbursement fund started by the Law Society of New Zealand in 1930 was widely publicized and discussed within Canada and the prestige of the measure increased markedly when the Law Society in England established the Compensation Fund in 1941. Once Alberta and Manitoba had established funds in Canada, and reported favourably on the effects, it became more difficult for the profession in other provinces to justify to representatives of the public their lack of such a public safeguard, and more difficult for the leaders of the profession to withstand the pressure from proponents within their ranks.

Once instituted, policies that are commitments to the public welfare appear to be irreversible. Like the welfare state, the profession that is given power in return for responsibility cannot easily revert to the simpler life by dropping collective services to the public. No outcry resulted when institutional advertising was abandoned precisely because it is defined in our society as self-interested behaviour; whereas, if a provincial bar were to bring to an end its reimbursement fund or free legal aid, the decision would be unfavourably regarded and difficult to defend. What may have been regarded originally as gratuitous acts tend with time to assume the status of obligations. The resolution of the current crisis in some provinces where large claims have exhausted the reimbursement funds and annual fees will have to be increased considerably if the funds are to be maintained,[41] will indicate whether this thesis is tenable.

Reimbursement funds and legal aid plans have been selected for discussion because the events surrounding their development provide an opportunity to delineate some of the social controls to which a self-governing profession is subject in our society. The sanctions we have discussed seem to bring public expectations and the interests of the profession into relationship in a way that makes for changes of policy in the direction of increased corporate responsibility for the public welfare. The depression years appear in retrospect to have been a period of ferment in which new ideas were generated and more members of the profession began to participate actively in the formulation of policies. Through numerous channels study, debate, and criticism took place on a wider scale than ever before. Many of the proposals were not translated into policy until a later period; this was the result, partly of the interval required for new ideas to gain sufficient acceptance and partly of the poor financial situation of the profession. World War II brought new prosperity but meant the postponement of new commitments. Towards the end of the war and immediately after, the stimulus to new measures was renewed by the prospect of less favourable conditions

[41] *The Financial Post*, Nov. 12, 1960.

for the profession. The return of many lawyers from the armed services, an influx of law students, and uncertainty about continued economic prosperity made steps to improve the standing of the profession seem important. In the period since then, facilitated by a relatively high level of income, most of the legal aid clinics and reimbursement funds have been established. An examination of changes in other fields of activity of the organized bar would reveal a similar pattern, but might also show that changes have taken place more slowly in matters of purely domestic concern which do not come to public view.

The Radical Political Movement in Canada

LEO ZAKUTA

"WHATEVER HAS HAPPENED to the C.C.F.?" The regularity with which the writer has been asked that question epitomizes its current problems. What the questioners have in mind—often indicated by the words which they accent—are the C.C.F.'s disappearance from the limelight and, less frequently, its sluggish manner and conventional viewpoint as compared with an earlier period. (The Co-operative Commonwealth Federation, a political party with a social democratic ideology, has been the dominant force in Canada's "left of centre" politics since its formation in 1933.)

The simplest answer to this question is to refer to the changes which have occurred in both the country and the party since 1933, suggesting that the public lost interest in the C.C.F. because of prosperity and welfare legislation and that the party became conservative and apathetic because as its members grew older and more prosperous they acquired other interests and responsibilities.

Although that answer has some validity, it is much too simple. It fails to explain why, of the many socialist parties which encountered these kinds of conditions, some grew large and serene and others remained inconsequential and fiercely at odds with "the world," while the C.C.F. took neither of these paths but became "worldly" despite its "failure." It is this unusual course of development by the C.C.F. that the present article undertakes to examine.

The C.C.F.'s worldliness is sufficiently visible in every aspect of its character[1] to suggest, at first glance, another answer to the origi-

---

[1] A party's "character" is used here to refer to its prevailing type of ideology, structure, and membership involvement. The process in which that character becomes more worldly is called by the familiar, if awkward, term "institutionalization." It refers to the sequence of changes in which a new crusading group tends to lose its original character as it becomes involved in "the world" and to become increasingly like the established worldly bodies against whose very nature it initially arose in protest.

nal question. As one steps away from the party and looks about at other organizations, one might well reply, "Nothing very remarkable has happened. The C.C.F. has simply gone the way of all, or at least of most, organizations."

Both the party and "the world" have indeed come a long way towards meeting each other since the birth of the C.C.F. The party's urge to "shatter to bits this sorry scheme of things entire" has grown feeble and its vision of the co-operative commonwealth into which the world would be remoulded become dim. The public and the "old parties" have come to accept many of its ideas which they had once rejected as unthinkable. The viewpoints of the party and "the world" are still some distance apart, but they have ceased to outrage one another. Indeed, that very convergence has become the most serious threat to the C.C.F.'s existence, though only because the party is so weak.

As the C.C.F.'s initial struggle for acceptance drew to an end, the usual changes occurred. The excitement subsided and the host of enthusiastic amateurs turned its main attention elsewhere (although most retained some allegiance), leaving the party's direction increasingly to the much smaller groups of professionals, attached to the central offices, which had begun to grow in the meantime. The latter have, however, gained influence not simply by default but because they are more deeply and fully involved. As professionals, their livelihood and entire careers are, of course, at stake, but, like their counterparts anywhere, they regard themselves as more competent than any amateur, however zealous, can be. They have developed techniques for the management of the organization that are geared to its more settled and less personal character. These methods include those which any professional group employs to cope with the fact that it is the amateurs who possess ultimate control of the organization.

Some of the amateurs continue to hold meetings, as they do in most voluntary organizations; but, as elsewhere, these meetings are less frequent, more sparsely attended, and almost exclusively devoted to conducting the "business" of the local branch. In fact, though not in form, they tend to treat fundamental policy as established and received rather than as "issues" which require local determination.[2] This description might apply, however roughly, to most groups

---

The institutionalization of the C.C.F. constitutes the main theme of the study of which this article is a part. See Leo Zakuta, "A Becalmed Protest Movement," unpublished Ph.D. thesis, University of Chicago, 1961.

[2] For a description of the corresponding groups in the British Labour party, see R. T. MacKenzie, *British Political Parties* (London, 1955), pp. 539-58.

which begin with a new and unacceptable idea—religious denominations, welfare bodies, and perhaps even business organizations—as
they and their members secure comfortable places in the world.
It was just this process in radical political movements that Michels
described so well and illustrated so profusely, though perhaps with
an excessive flavour of disenchantment and of exposé.[3]

What makes the C.C.F. distinctive, however, is that it has been
acquiring the qualities described above without having achieved a
comparable place in society and, indeed, while it has been losing the
modest position which it had attained.[4] In brief, its character has
grown more worldly while its position has been becoming more
precarious. This combination of character and position departs not
only from the pattern of socialist and other parties but also from the
conventional institutionalization cycle suggested by Dawson and
Gettys,[5] which presumably applies much more widely. However, to
explain this departure it is first necessary to show how political parties differ from other organizations and, then, how minor parties
differ from both political movements and major parties. In the light
of that analysis, the distinctive place of the C.C.F. in the socialist
world becomes more apparent and more comprehensible.

Political Parties[6] and Other Organizations

All organizations whose membership is predominantly voluntary,
including political parties, share certain hazards and conditions of
existence which differentiate them from non-voluntary bodies. The
chief one is harnessing their membership in the absence of some of
the main devices that are available to other types of organizations.
Because voluntary members are not subject to the usual bread-and-
butter incentives, these groups must do without this central mecha-
nism of human control. Instead, they depend all the more heavily
on their members' inner convictions and concern about the approval
of their fellows so that a weakening of either is particularly damag-
ing to voluntary groups. At best, regular routines of work and participation are difficult to establish in organizations of this type and

[3] Robert Michels, *Political Parties* (Glencoe, Ill., 1949).
[4] "Position" is used throughout to refer to the group's strength, as determined by popular support, rather than to an ideological stand.
[5] C. A. Dawson, and Warner E. Gettys, *An Introduction to Sociology* (3rd ed.; New
York, 1948), pp. 689-709.
[6] It should be understood that the entire discussion of political groups applies only
where elections are free.

are, therefore, often sources of anxious preoccupation. (Frequently the group devotes much effort and money to mobilizing its voluntary members as a necessary preliminary, with the public as ultimate target.)

Although political parties share these problems with all voluntary organizations, they nevertheless encounter special ones of their own in attempting to secure and hold a clientele and membership. Every group faces uncertainties when its clientele is free to choose whom it will patronize, and competition for a clientele is, of course, the common lot, extending far beyond voluntary organizations. In politics, however, the conditions of that competition are unique in ways that create a special relation between the party and its clientele, the electorate. The distinctive feature is that, of all organizations which provide goods and services, only political parties cannot (legally) offer these in direct return for patronage (votes). The reason is, of course, not only that the ballot is secret, but that only the winner(s), by controlling the government, is in a position to fulfil any obligations. (One can argue, however, that any party which makes a significant show of strength may indirectly provide a return to its patrons.)

Because winning is so important, the services of a political party are, unlike those of other organizations, widely sought only if the party is already very popular or is apparently becoming so. (This accounts for most of the difficulties encountered by new parties and for the special importance of the "bandwagon" in politics.) In more familiar terms, many a voter concludes that his ballot would be "wasted" if it is cast for a party which he feels has "no chance." Consequently, if he votes at all, he is likely to do so for a party which he likes less but whose seemingly superior prospects make him feel that his vote is not meaningless. This tendency obviously contributes significantly to the stability of the political system by helping to keep the major parties strong and the minor ones weak. Therefore, unless a political party appears to be "going somewhere," it is unlikely to maintain even a steady level of existence. Because other kinds of organizations can prosper or at least maintain a stable clientele without having any prospect of overtaking their larger rivals, they can lead more settled and less hazardous lives than can political parties.

In a major party, however, these uncertainties are counterbalanced by the numerous ballots which it obtains from people who do not regard it as their first preference but vote for it nevertheless, because

they wish either to remove its main rival from office or else to prevent it from getting there. This tendency is sufficiently extensive to
make most major parties seem virtually indestructible.

Minor Parties and Other Political Organizations

The position of minor parties, however, deprives them of this form
of built-in insurance, and, except where they are protected by the
proportional representation system,[7] they have a much higher mortality rate than do major parties or radical political movements.
Several conditions make minor parties far more susceptible to the
rule of "up or out" than are other political as well as non-political
organizations.

The first is that the special relation, described above, between a
political party and the electorate also exists, although the details
differ, between the party and its own members. The members invest
far more in the party than do the voters, giving it some combination
of their energy, time, devotion, money, or possibly career. To realize
a return on that investment, they must regard the party as a potential
winner. If not, they are likely to question the value of their investment and to transfer it elsewhere. Though the time span which they
employ may be longer than the public's, and they usually obtain
other rewards, the fundamental similarity of the relation remains.
Thus the decisions of the members and officers of a political party
resemble those of investors. The study of any particular party
reveals how greatly the contribution or withdrawal of the invest-
ments of members and officers (and not only the support of voters)
can affect the party's fortunes and how much such action depends
on the hope of *winning* the contest of popularity.

The preceding discussion has suggested that minor parties owe
their high mortality rate to the readiness with which the public loses
interest in them and their own members lose heart. This link be-

---

[7] The proportional representation system, which is so prevalent in Europe, is much
kinder to minor parties and less helpful to major ones than is the system which prevails
in the English-speaking world. (Indeed it tends to make the distinctions between
"major" and "minor" less clear than they usually are under the latter system.) These
facts account both for the multiplicity of parties where proportional representation is
used and for the high correlation between the strength of parties and their attitudes
towards these two types of electoral systems.

The remainder of this discussion deals with minor parties in the simple-plurality,
single-ballot system. (For a detailed discussion of how that system affects political
parties and especially the minor ones, see Maurice Duverger, *Political Parties*, translated by Barbara and Robert North [London, 1954]).

tween a party's survival chances, on the one hand, and its character and position, on the other, becomes clearer when the minor parties are compared in these respects to major parties and to political protest movements which have not yet taken on a party character.

Ideologically, the minor parties are in a difficult position. Political protest movements usually possess a clearer *raison d'être* in their highly distinctive viewpoint. The major parties, though rather alike in viewpoint because their strength and proximity to power make them representative of and sensitive to many shades of public opinion, nevertheless, also possess a more obvious self-justification than do the minor parties—the possession or imminent prospect of power.

Each of these positions provides an effective basis for claiming support from the public as well as from party ranks. Political protest movements demand support on the grounds of a transcendental moral justification rather than on the grounds of impending victory. Major parties are less outraged by the state of things and less utopian in their promises, but they seek support on the grounds of their immediate prospect of holding office. Both of these positions provide obvious, if very different, justifications for existence in the struggle for political survival.

The position of the minor parties is uneasy, by contrast, because they cannot press either of these claims for support very effectively. When "the world" has ceased to outrage them and their visions of utopia have grown faint, they can do little more than intone the rituals of crusade. For example, much of the fear and anger which the depression aroused in the C.C.F. was mellowed or perhaps anaesthetized by the continued post-war prosperity; simultaneously, the immediate rather than the distant future became the party's main concern. In addition, their remoteness from power renders the other claim for support virtually unusable.

Establishing a *raison d'être* which is both comprehensible and compelling seems to be an inherent problem of minor parties. The difficulty becomes compounded in times of blurred doctrinal differences, such as the present, and when, like the C.C.F., the minor party must search for a place within a cherished two-party system.

Structurally, minor parties occupy an intermediate position between the proselytizing movements which are more personal and tightly knit and the major parties which are held together more loosely and formally. Although the minor parties are more firmly planted in "the world" than are the proselytizing movements, they are less deeply and intricately rooted in it than are the major parties.

If the C.C.F.'s case is typical, the minor party's membership may be greater than it was in the earlier, more sectarian period. But a larger proportion of it is less involved, maintaining little more than a formal connection with the party and refusing to be stirred into active participation, despite all of the party's efforts.[8] (The importance of the large, inactive membership should not be underestimated. It provides the party with much of its money and perseverance, the latter because of the constant hope that this "sleeping giant" can be awakened.) The efforts to do so, however, like most of the organization's activities, come increasingly under the direction of a hierarchy of paid officers who develop more formal ways of carrying on the party's affairs.

The kind of structure described above is, of course, even more characteristic of the major parties. But the latter can be stirred with greater ease and, once aroused, they reach farther. The stimulant is the anticipation of holding office; while their organizations are more effective because of their greater size and range of connections in the community, proximity to power enables them to marshal leaders and followers, candidates and funds, both from their own ranks and from other groups.

Emotionally, the minor party cannot draw heavily on either the motive power which drives a crusading movement or that which feeds a major party. Fear and indignation are the chief ingredients of the former, and utopian hopes are the sparks which ignite them. These elements cannot exist without a menacing set of villains (for example, capitalism's inherent depressions and a tendency towards fascism) and a stirring vision of the future (an abundant and classless society, for instance). But as the minor party's villain and vision recede, so does the energy which they generate.

Despite their growing resemblance to their major rivals, the minor parties cannot harness the latter's main source of energy either. Its chief ingredient is the anticipation of worldly achievements, both personal and otherwise, and the igniting agent is the prospect of impending victory. The feebleness of that prospect naturally deprives the minor parties of most of this motive power.

In summary, minor parties differ from political movements and major parties in the following ways: their *raison d'être* is less distinct

[8] For a study of the difficulties experienced by some minor American parties in maintaining membership loyalty and participation, see W. Kornhauser, "Organizationa Loyalty: A Study of Liberal and Radical Political Careers," unpublished Ph.D. thesis University of Chicago, 1953.

than the former's, but less workable than the latter's, their organizations are more formal and firmly rooted in "the world" than the former's but less so than the latter's; and their members are less involved than the former's but less easily activated than the latter's. Minor parties are thus closer in position to political movements and closer in character to major parties. But the former owe their survival chiefly to their character and the latter to their position. In other words, minor parties resemble each of these other groups most in that aspect which contributes least to these other groups' survival.

It would be misleading to conclude that minor parties live in the worst of all possible worlds; the C.C.F., for example, still draws more support than it did in its initial phase. But these parties have lost the protest movement's sustaining faith in the inevitability of ultimate triumph without being in a position to acquire the major party's assurance of taking office as soon as the public tires of its main rival.

These conditions account for the special susceptibility to the rule of "up or out" of those lesser political groups whose character comes to resemble that of the old and secure members of the establishment. They further indicate how difficult it is for these groups to achieve a secure place in society, compared to most non-political organizations of similar size and worldliness. This difference, in turn, leads to differences in character. The C.C.F.'s viewpoint, for example, is plagued by doubt and uncertainty as the party searches for a new *raison d'être* and its organization has been steadily enfeebled by the extensive demoralization which, in manifold forms, has spread throughout it.

The C.C.F. and Other Socialist Parties

We can now return to the question of why the C.C.F., although unsuccessful, nonetheless acquired a worldly character. That combination, although rare in the socialist world, is not uncommon among minor parties. However, the question remains: Why did the C.C.F. not become either a major, worldly party or an inconsequential, other-worldly sect?

One might argue that only those socialist parties which achieved a minimal degree of momentum fairly early in their careers were able to achieve major party status by the democratic process. The evidence for this argument is that every one of the social democratic parties which did attain that momentum climbed steadily to power

or to its threshold and remained a major party. The failure of the
United States Socialist party, on the other hand, might be attributed
to its inability to achieve that minimal degree of propulsion.[9]

Whatever the plausibility of this argument, it obviously does
not apply to the C.C.F. The latter acquired as much momentum,
in the early 1940's (Table I), as any socialist party ever had, but its

TABLE I

C.C.F. POPULAR SUPPORT IN CANADA, 1940-5 *

	Party Percentages				
Date	C.C.F.	Lib.	Cons.	Bloc Populaire	Others
1940 Mar. (election)	9	55	31		5
1942 Jan.	10	55	30		5
Sept.	21	39	23		17
1943 Feb.	23	32	27	7	11
Sept.	29	28	28	9	6
1944 Jan.	24	30	29	9	8
Sept.	24	36	27	5	8
1945 Jan.	22	36	28	6	8
June (election)	16	41	28	3	12

*Gallup Poll, reported in Dean. E. McHenry, *The Third Force in Canada* (Berkeley and
Los Angeles, 1950), p. 136.

progress was quite uncharacteristically arrested and abruptly reversed, and it failed to establish itself as a major party. In view of its
departure from so ubiquitous a pattern, that failure gives a final
twist to the query of "whatever happened to the C.C.F.?" Why was
the pattern reversed so sharply in Canada, and only there, once it
had got so well under way?

The most obvious explanation of this failure seems to lie in the
general political system which Canada shares with most of the
English-speaking world. That system, we have observed, does not
provide comfortable accommodation for more than two parties at a
time. New parties, because of their regional bases, have challenged
its established tenants more successfully in the provincial field than
in the federal. (At present, 1960, Canada's three most westerly provinces are in Social Credit or C.C.F. hands.) But the dominance of

[9] At the height of its popularity, in 1912, the Socialist party won only 6 per cent of the
presidential vote and only one seat in Congress. Since then it has been sidelined in all
but name from the main political arena.

the Liberals and Conservatives nationally has remained unbroken since Confederation.

Despite several attempts, no other party has ever won federal power. The C.C.F. and Social Credit have been the most recent and, in an important sense, the most unusual aspirants to that goal. Other new parties have been either popular or persistent, but never both. Some, like the Progressive party of the early 1920's or the Reconstruction party of the mid-1930's, blossomed suddenly and even spectacularly, but faded almost as rapidly—the common fate of most new parties that originate by splitting off from the established major ones.[10] Other political groups, such as the Communists, the Trotskyites (despite several splinterings), and the followers of Daniel de Leon, have survived for decades on the dark outer fringes of the political scene. Only the C.C.F. and Social Credit were able to combine popularity with durability, and even the latter was virtually obliterated as a national party in the 1958 federal election. Nevertheless, the success of other social democratic parties, and particularly of the British Labour party, is decisive evidence that small, third parties are not inevitably doomed to that status, and such success suggests that the formal political system does not in itself account adequately for the C.C.F.'s weak position.

There are, of course, substantial differences between the history and character of Canada and other countries which are reflected in the differences between the C.C.F. and socialist parties elsewhere. For example, unlike most of its European counterparts, the C.C.F. arrived on the scene too late to participate in the main battles for political liberty, the franchise and trade union legitimacy. The fact that these goals had been achieved, as a consequence of North America's special conditions, was undoubtedly responsible for the C.C.F.'s late start and for its lack of a massive trade union base, both of which have handicapped it severely, although neither seems to have been an insurmountable obstacle in itself.

Although all of the major socialist parties, those in the new nations excepted, were formed by the beginning of the twentieth

[10] In origin and type of life cycle these parties have less in common with the C.C.F. than with such third parties in the United States as the Bull Moose, the two Progressive, and the Dixiecrat. These also began by springing full-bodied from the major parties, following unsuccessful efforts to win control of them, disintegrated after only one genuine trial of strength, and were largely reabsorbed by their original parties.

The Canadian Progressive Party had a somewhat more independent origin and, after disintegrating, its radical minority was instrumental in founding the C.C.F. See W. L. Morton, *The Progressive Party in Canada* (Toronto, 1950).

century, age by itself has not guaranteed success, as the United States Socialist party[11] and others demonstrate. Nor have formal alliances (collective affiliations) with trade unions been essential to the success of socialist parties, as the evidence from continental Europe indicates.[12] But the socialist parties which did succeed seem to have obtained the votes of the great majority of industrial workers. The C.C.F.'s failure to obtain these votes and match these successes has been attributed by F. H. Underhill and others to the distinctive conditions of political life in North America.

... socialism [in Canada]... was obviously an importation, partly from Marxians in continental Europe, and partly from the more moderate parliamentary socialists, the Fabian socialists, of England. It obviously didn't originate in Canada; the C.C.F. was an attempt to adapt these European ideas, primarily the Fabian ideas, to Canadian conditions.
... I feel the C.C.F. was an attempt to set up a British-type of party system, a division between left and right. We [the C.C.F.] were defeated by Mr. King because he was a good North American and he saw that our politics wasn't likely to work that way.[13]

The efforts to explain the C.C.F.'s failure call attention to its "environment," the examination of which is a task beyond the scope of the present paper and one which obviously requires a different type of investigation. But, however much the special North American or Canadian environment may explain the party's weakness, it cannot account adequately for the C.C.F.'s departure from the usual paths taken by political movements which have felt decisively rejected. Its fate was especially unusual for North America where re-

[11] The Socialist party, although formed in 1902, only two years after the British Labour party, is very much weaker than even the C.C.F.
[12] Formal collective affiliation exists only in the Swedish and Norwegian parties and, in both cases, only on the local level, in contrast to the practice in the British Labour party. In Norway, these affiliations constitute only about 35 per cent of the present Labour party membership. (For a more detailed discussion of these arrangements and of the main types of relations between the trade unions and the socialist parties of the democratic nations of continental Europe, see "Structural Relationships between Trade Unions and Labour Parties," a series of three articles by Paul Malles, Assistant to the Director of Organization, I.C.F.T.U., in *Canadian Labour*, Oct., Nov., and Dec. 1959.)
[13] F. H. Underhill, "The Radical Tradition: A Second View of Canadian History," published transcript of two broadcasts on the CBC Television Series, Explorations, June 8 and 15, 1960 (CBC Publications, Toronto). See Morton, *The Progressive Party in Canada* p. 270, for a similar explanation of the Progressive party's failure. These views leave unexplained, however, the fact that the C.C.F. did come very close to power or to becoming Canada's second party. The timing of its upsurge, several years before the next election was due to be held, undoubtedly played a large part in its failure to achieve either of these objectives.

form parties, if unsuccessful, tend to collapse and blow away or shrink into purely regional groups, and where radical movements, if the climate is uninviting, seem to shrivel and crawl back into a hard, sectarian shell.

Any of these developments would have been more typical of an unsuccessful political movement than the one that did take place. The C.C.F. did not collapse; neither did it dwindle into a spent sect or a purely regional party. Instead, as a minor national party[14] it has retained and developed the worldly character which had blossomed during its period of great expansion.

If nurture alone fails to account for this distinctive combination, then nature must be added. An examination of the members of the C.C.F.'s general ideological family reveals their "natural" processes of change and clarifies how and why the C.C.F. has departed from these patterns. To illuminate that departure more fully both the established and the unwordly socialist parties must be considered.

THE C.C.F. AND THE MAJOR SOCIALIST PARTIES

A comparison of the growth of the C.C.F. and of its major relatives reveals one significant difference.[15] Once the latter had attained the level of popularity reached by the C.C.F. in the early 1940's, none suffered a serious reversal before becoming safely established as the first or second party in the land.[16] Thus when they eventually met defeat, they still remained the chief alternatives to the parties in power. (Many of them had already held or shared office.)

How significant this difference was becomes apparent if one compares the process of change within the C.C.F. and these other parties. Although the character of the C.C.F. changed remarkably during the party's brief interlude of success,[17] the main changes to more conventional forms occurred after June 1945, while the party was

[14] Although the C.C.F.'s strength in the five most easterly provinces is negligible, it has retained sufficient support in the rest of the country to qualify as a national party.
[15] For a record of the popular support of these parties, see Leo Zakuta, "A Becalmed Protest Movement," Appendix B.
[16] To appreciate the magnitude of the C.C.F.'s double defeat (in Ontario and federally) in June 1945, one should not compare these results with those of pre-1942 elections. One should contrast them instead with the 1943 returns in Ontario, with the 1944 victory in Saskatchewan, with the sequence of by-election victories, with the Gallup Poll reports and, above all, with the soaring hopes and imaginations of C.C.F. supporters upon the eve of these 1945 contests.
[17] The period of rising popular support lasted less than two years, achieving its high-water mark by September, 1943, while that of organizational expansion endured little more than three years, ending abruptly in June, 1945.

still reeling from defeat with its popular support, membership, and revenues shrinking steadily.

In contrast, the major socialist parties had developed their more conventional viewpoints, incentives, and organizations during long periods of steady growth which frequently included tenure of office. When their progress was finally reversed, they had already secured a new *modus vivendi*—as established alternatives to the parties in power, a position which insured them heavily against the hazards of defeat and change. When defeat forced the members of these parties to recognize that they were participating in the conventional political process rather than in an irreversible crusade, the prospect of forming the next government continued to arouse them to action. That same prospect provided an effective and easily understood *raison d'être* when their socialism became less clear and ardent. And it enabled these parties to hold together in defeat the organizations and the alliances which they had built during their long and steady rise.

The C.C.F., in contrast, was badly hurt by the combination of defeat and change. (Tables II and III).[18] Defeat led to hopelessness which sapped the energies of many members and deflated the interest of the public. And when the early faith in utopian socialism withered, no stimulating *raison d'être* was available to replace it. Consequently, these twin losses—of hope in present victory and of certainty in ultimate triumph—inflicted fatal or critical injuries on much of the party's organization. They left the C.C.F. neither a major party nor a political movement, defeat demolishing the former and change the latter role.

It is in these respects that the "natural" processes of institutionali-

TABLE II

NATIONAL ELECTIONS, 1935-1958: SEATS WON BY PARTIES*

Party	1935	1940	1945	1949	1953	1957	1958
Liberal	171	178	125	190	170	105	49
Conservative	39	39	67	41	51	111	208
C.C.F.	7	8	28	13	23	25	8
Social Credit	17	10	13	10	15	19	0
Others	11	10	12	8	6	5	0
TOTALS	245	245	245	262	265	265	265

* *Canadian Parliamentary Guide.*

[18] The reversals of 1945 had left it Canada's third party, much weaker than its two main rivals and very remote from power.

TABLE III

NATIONAL ELECTIONS, 1935-1958: PERCENTAGE OF POPULAR VOTE, BY PARTIES

Party	1935	1940	1945	1949	1953	1957	1958
Liberal	44	55	41	50	49	40	33
Conservative	30	31	28	30	31	40	54
C.C.F.	9	9	16	13	12	11	10
Social Credit	4	3	4	2	5	6	2
Others	13	2	10	5	4	3	1
TOTALS	100	100	99	100	101	100	100

zation have taken so unusual a course in the C.C.F. Instead of following the typical protest movement–minor party–major party sequence of its stronger socialist confreres, the C.C.F's career more nearly approximates a sequence of protest movement–major party–minor party. This unusual sequence of rise and decline appears to have twisted the C.C.F. out of the more familiar socialist forms. The essential difference was not that the C.C.F. was catapulted into "the world" and became deeply involved in it—this happened to many socialist parties. Instead, it was that, although the party experienced a profound change of character during its middle (major party) phase,[19] it failed to establish a secure place in that world. Had it done so, as it fully expected to, it would have resembled its major relatives in position as well as in character.

THE C.C.F. AND THE MINOR SOCIALIST GROUPS

If its position distinguishes the C.C.F. from the major socialist parties, its character separates it from the lesser groups of the "left." These groups are much less involved in the struggle for power and have retained much more of their sectarian character, adding to it only the qualities common to those political groups which the public has never taken seriously.

Even the United States Socialist party might be placed in this category. Its distinctive features in the past two decades have been its other-worldliness and insignificance in the struggle for power, both of which it shares with numerous other "left wing" groups. Many of these other groups have either repudiated or not been concerned with the more conventional forms of the struggle for power. Instead,

---

[19] The C.C.F. regarded itself as almost a major party and was so regarded by the public and the other parties until the federal election of 1949 made its minor party status unmistakeable. The changes in its character during this phase are described in detail in Leo Zakuta, "A Becalmed Political Movement," chaps. VI-IX.

much more than the C.C.F. ever did, they have rejected the world and looked towards an entirely new and utopian social order, awaiting the cataclysm which would usher it in and provide the opportunity and the necessity for their leadership.

There are still other socialist (and non-socialist) groups which are essentially parties-in-exile but which have little hope or desire to return to the scene of their original endeavours. They maintain their ideology and some aspects of their structure with surprisingly little change. But their stability also stems from the absence of a deep involvement in the issues of here and now. However, instead of dwelling in the remote future, their hearts live in the past and in another place. The Communist party also looks elsewhere, a fact which governs most of its behaviour, including its time perspective.

THE C.C.F.'S DISTINCTIVE PLACE IN THE SOCIALIST WORLD

Their perspectives of time and place seem to divide the socialist and other "left wing" parties in the democratic countries into two broad categories which correspond closely to their strength (position). The first consists of the parties whose main concern is with the present and with their immediate surroundings; most of these are large and powerful. The other category contains the parties whose primary orientation is to another time or place or both and, except for the Communist party in Italy, France, and pre-Nazi Germany, they have been small and weak.

In which category does the C.C.F. belong? Its character has become close to that of the major socialist parties, but it increasingly lacks their secure status. Its position, on the contrary, has been nearing that of the minor socialist groups (although it is very much stronger than any of them), but it increasingly lacks their sectarian character. Thus the C.C.F.'s main distinction appears to be that it has been developing the character of a major party while moving towards the position of a minor sect. In the terms used previously, the C.C.F.'s strength and its perspectives of time and place seem to be heading in opposite directions. It is this unusual relation between them, for which the party's peculiar pattern of success and failure is chiefly responsible, that creates the impression of a disparity between the C.C.F.'s position and character.

One may ask why the C.C.F. did not return to its original character after its reversals. The answer lies in the depth of its (and its members') involvement in the conventional world as well as in the state of the latter since the war. Although the world has been hard on the party, it has been much kinder to its individual members and to the public at large. A drastic change on the broader Canadian scene might have led either the existing leaders and members to reject the social order once again and to recapture the character of a militant political movement or to a wholesale turnover of personnel with the same result.[20] Since that change in the environment did not occur, the C.C.F. retained its worldly character despite a weakening position.

The C.C.F.'s Prospects

One cannot help wondering how long the C.C.F. can keep riding these two horses, character and position, if they keep travelling in opposite directions, without being torn asunder. The answer seems to hinge on two main possibilities, the arrival of strong trade union reinforcements and a drastic change in the political climate from that of the past decade and a half. These possibilities constitute the party's chief sources of continued hope.

But if neither of these events materializes, or perhaps if only the latter does, the C.C.F. may follow the path taken by the United States Socialist party after the peaks of strength it rose to in 1912 and 1932. If a leader emerges with the magnetic appeal of a Woodrow Wilson or a Franklin Roosevelt or, as seems more likely in the Canadian political system, if a sufficiently decisive issue arises, one of the major parties may draw off a substantial segment of the C.C.F., those whose views have moved farthest into "the world." The distance that these people would have to travel is no longer very great, and they might find themselves in the same position as the Socialist party stalwarts who became supporters of the New Deal.

The other horse could then ride off unfettered in the opposite direction, carrying a handful of the more militant and utopian of the C.C.F.'s followers. Thus, by reducing the party to a fraction of its present strength and returning its time perspective to the more remote future, such a development would restore the "natural" order of the socialist world. It is partly to ward off just such an eventuality that the leaders of the C.C.F. are now striving so desperately to build a "new party."

[20] For a description of just such a change in the United States Socialist party in the early 1930's, see Daniel Bell, "Marxian Socialism [in the United States]," in *Socialism and American Life*, ed. by D. D. Egbert and S. Persons (Princeton, 1952).

The formation of the C.C.F. in 1932-3 resulted from the same kind of influx in personnel and change in character of the Canadian socialist movement at exactly the same period.